CW01459181

CANINE
CRIMEBUSTERS

CANINE
CRIMEBUSTERS

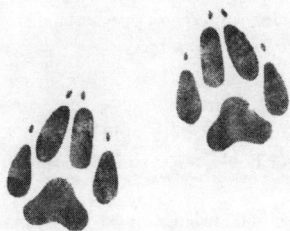

ANDY BOOT

m
B
MIRROR BOOKS

m
B

MIRROR BOOKS

All of the events in this story are true, but some names and
details have been changed to protect the identities
of individuals.

© Andy Boot

The rights of Andy Boot to be identified as the author of this
book have been asserted, in accordance with the Copyright,
Designs and Patents Act 1988.

All rights reserved. No part of this publication may be
reproduced, stored in a retrieval system, or transmitted,
in any form or by any means without the prior written
permission of the publisher, nor be otherwise circulated in
any form of binding or cover other than that in which it is
published and without a similar condition being imposed on
the subsequent purchaser.

1

Published in Great Britain and Ireland in 2025 by
Mirror Books, a Reach PLC business.

Photographic Acknowledgements: Mirrorpix, Alamy

www.mirrorbooks.co.uk
@TheMirrorBooks

Print ISBN 9781917439190
eBook ISBN 9781917439206

Editing and Production: Christine Costello
Cover Design: Chris Collins

Printed and bound in Great Britain by
CPI Group (UK) Ltd, Croydon, CR0 4YY

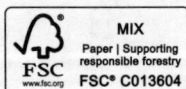

FSC
www.fsc.org

MIX
Paper | Supporting
responsible forestry
FSC® C013604

for Anita, Rambo and Winnie, and for all those who care for the working dogs and their welfare when that working life is over

CONTENTS

Timeline   8
Foreword   13
Prologue   15

PART ONE: Early Days of Police Dogs

Introduction   20
The Four Dogs Of The Apocalypse   34
Jim: A Police Dog's Vocation   60

PART TWO: Dogs in a Post World War Two Era

Rex III: the Archetype of a Police Dog   88

PART THREE: Late 20th Century Police Work

Major: The Quarry, The Thief and the Wardrobe 144

PART FOUR : The New Millennium

New Era, New Advances   178
Taz: The Cost Of Duty   186
Zippy: Sniffing And Snapping   227

Epilogue   267
Acknowledgements   271

Timeline

POLICE DOG Sections as we think of them now did not generally form until after World War Two. However, there were initial programmes and some activity in the 80 years prior to the end of the war. There were also maverick uses of dogs, down to the whims of individuals and sometimes the dogs themselves.

1860s: Constable Edward Barrett uses his own dog as an unofficial police dog in Launceston, Cornwall.

1883: Also in Cornwall, Truro Police Supt. Edward Marshall uses his own dog.

1889: Chief Constable Charles Warren of the Metropolitan Force brings bloodhounds into the hunt for Jack The Ripper with disastrous results.

1890s: Topper, an Airedale, becomes first 'official' police dog for the Met, stationed at Hyde Park, but more of a publicity stunt than a working dog.

1895: Major Edwin Richardson, ex-Army and a dog trainer for ambulance services starts to train dogs with a view to use by the Police.

1897: Plymouth Police are gifted the St Bernard 'Colonel' by his owner, as he keeps following policemen about town.

1899: In Ghent, police dogs are first used in an organised manner in Europe, followed by Prussia in 1901.

TIMELINE

1902-11: Terrier Jack is adopted by the Constable patrolling Devonport Dockyard and is an unofficial police dog, even gifted a pension when he goes blind and is retired in his last year.

1906: Major Ricardson approaches the Met with his idea of Police dogs, to be met with muted interest.

1908: Hertford County Constabulary agree in principle to a pilot programme with Major Richardson.

1908: November – the British Northeastern Railway Police introduce the first dog unit in the UK when they deploy Mick, Jim, Vick and Ben, four Airedales, under the direction of Inspector Dobie following discussion with Hull Docks Manager Mr Geddes, who lobbied for dogs after witnessing them in use in Ghent.

1910: Other Railway Police Units across the country take up the use of dogs following success at Hull. Glasgow trial Police dogs, working with Major Richardson and using his specially developed Executive breed.

1911: The Chief Constable of Liverpool buys the first dogs for the force from Major Richardson as part of a trial scheme. Hertford continue to prevaricate with Major Richardson, their posited new trial programme stalled with disagreement about breed of dog to be used.

1914: Exeter Chief Constable Arthur Nicholson gifts his Airedale to a Constable on his force, to aid on patrol.

1923: The newly amalgamated British Transport Police open the first dedicated Police dog training unit at Inmans Farm, Heddon Hall, Hull. In Bristol, Airedale Jim attaches himself to his local station and becomes first unofficial police dog for the Bristol Constabulary.

1930s: In Devon bloodhounds are an unofficial part of the 'escape plan' squad established for break-outs from Dartmoor Prison.

1933: Following this, Devon discusses the setting up of a dog unit. Det Insp Tom Roberts of the Surrey force establishes a trial programme with bloodhounds, referring back to his experiences with these dogs as a young officer.

1934: A Home Office Committee is established to report on possible widespread dog use in the Police.

1938: First Met Police trials with two labradors.

1939: Walsall introduce Don as the first Midlands Police dog.

1946: Met force opens first dog section, using labradors, based at Imber Court, primarily the centre for Police horse training.

1946: The now Supt. Tom Roberts continues to lobby his Surrey Force about dogs. In new Chief Constable Joseph Simpson, who breeds and trains dogs with his wife, he finds an ally. They discuss breeds and make research trips to Belgium and Germany.

1948: Recruiting Harry Darbyshire, a dog trainer and Constable in the Met who favours Alsatians over labradors, and so is told there is no place for him in the Met Dog Section, they promote him to Sergeant and station him in a house with a garden in Shackleford to begin a training programme.

1949: The results of the initial programme are so successful that the new Surrey Dog Section is established at the newly built Surrey Police Headquarters at Mount Browne, where Darbyshire creates a training and breeding programme that is the blueprint for Dog Section development in the rest of the country.

1950: Met introduce Alsatians for the first time, spurred by success of Surrey programme.

1951: Birmingham introduce their first police dog, Flash.

1952: Hampshire introduce their first police dogs via the Southampton Force, with dogs purchased from Surrey.

1953: Dyfed-Powys Police form the first Welsh Police Dog Section. Official formation of City Of Glasgow Police Dog Branch. Essex Police Dog Section formed with Remoh (a Doberman) and Senta (an Alsatian) purchased from Surrey.

1954: The Met move their dog section headquarters from Imber Court to Keston. Having learned from the loss of Harry Darbyshire and their errors over Alsatians, Keston becomes on a par with Mount Browne as the premier dog training and breeding unit in the UK.

1955: Twenty-two years after discussions begin, Devon finally establishes its Dog Unit.

1957: Portsmouth becomes the second force in Hampshire to use dogs.

1957: First official Bristol Police Dog Section, with the introduction of Kyloe and Kudos, Alsatians bought from Surrey.

1959: Cornwall propose the formation of a Dog Unit.

1961: Coventry recruit their first three dogs – Flame, Blaze and Dante – named in memory of the firebombing of the City in World War Two.

1964: Cornwall Constabulary Dog Section formed.

1968: The Prison Service establish their own dog section: prior to this, all dogs and handlers for use in prisons were provided by the local police force.

Foreword

BY THE RT. HON. THE COUNTESS
BATHURST

THERE ARE few partnerships as remarkable as that of a police dog and handler. Together, they stand as an unshakable team – one built on trust, loyalty, and an unbreakable bond.

These courageous dogs dedicate their lives to protecting the public, tracking down criminals, searching for the lost and vulnerable, and detecting dangerous substances that threaten our safety. Whether they are trained in general purpose policing, searching for drugs, cash, weapons, or even detecting human remains, each of these incredible animals plays a vital role in keeping our communities safe.

The history of police dogs dates back more than a century, with early records of their use in law enforcement stretching back to the early 20th century. From those first police dogs Jim, Vic, Ben, and Mick patrolling the docks in Hull, to the highly skilled teams we see today, the evolution of these remarkable animals has been driven by their intelligence, dedication, and unwavering courage. Their instincts, paired with extensive training, make them one of the most valuable assets to policing across the world.

But a police dog is never alone in their mission. Behind every brave dog is a devoted handler – one who trains, guides, and trusts their four-legged partner with their life.

This is more than a working relationship; it is a partnership based on mutual respect and an understanding that, no matter the challenge, they face it together. Through every chase, every search, and every moment of danger, they move as one, each protecting the other in ways words can never truly capture.

As we honour these extraordinary animals, we also extend our deepest gratitude to their handlers. It is their dedication, skill, and compassion that allow their beloved K9s to thrive in their roles.

The bond they share goes beyond the job – it lasts a lifetime. And when these dogs retire, it is often their handlers who continue to care for them, ensuring they live out their well-earned retirement with the love and dignity they so richly deserve, which is why I am so proud to write the foreword to this wonderful book. As founder of the National Foundation for Retired Service Animals, I know all too well the, sometimes ultimate, sacrifice they make for us every day.

This book is a tribute to them all – the courageous police dogs, the handlers who stand beside them, and the unbreakable teams they form.

Their stories of bravery, skill, and service deserve to be told, and it is our privilege to share them with you. I hope you enjoy every word and every tale, as they mirror police dogs across the country. I am immensely proud of them all and to be a part of this story.

The Rt. Hon. The Countess Bathurst

Prologue

OUT OF THE DARKNESS...

IT WAS hard to work in the dark, but they could not risk light. The heavy clouds scudded over the starless sky, moon hidden by a low fog, with no light to reflect across the waters that were almost still, the only sound the creak of barges and slow, deep rattle of anchor chains straining in the tide. A lookout kept guard for them, though his use was limited in the all-encompassing gloom.

Sound was his job: the noise of the homeless who tried to eke a living and shelter on the docks should not stray too near while his fellow thieves were at work. The police patrols, themselves hampered by the necessity to work in the dark and so not carry lamps, shuffled, coughed, and landed heavy boots on the stones that gave a clue to how far they might be.

The gangs of thieves who haunted the docks worked under difficult conditions, having to break down the cargo they were stealing into easily transportable amounts, unable to risk bringing carts or barrows. They may have been able to use the police need for darkness in their favour, but navigating between the dark masses of crates with iron-rimmed wheels sparking on the stone was a risk too far.

These gangs worked hard for the cargo they pilfered: the goods may fetch them a tidy resale from the pubs and fences that were their markets, but they paid the price in sweat. The sweat that came from the hard slog of freeing their stolen goods from the crates and moving them off the dock; the sweat that came from constantly looking over their shoulder as they worked; the threat of a police patrol always an unavoidable constant.

For several years now they had waged a war that was evenly matched. The police worked in the dark and on foot. The gangs worked in the dark and on foot.

That was about to change. On this night, as the gang worked on gathering their stolen goods, there was something different in the air. The lookout could hear something approaching at speed: a skittering footfall on the stone, rapid. How many feet? It sounded like an animal… no, more than one… but there had never been any horses on the dock after dark, and these sounds were not hooves.

Before he had a chance to call to his comrades and warn them, he could hear breathing, rapid and almost snorting, upon him. A low growl warned him as he stepped back. He felt something – no, more than one thing – brush past him at speed, knocking him off balance.

There was something beside him now, hot breath on his face. He put out a hand and felt what seemed to be a heavy, thick material and not the fur and flesh that he might expect. He tried to call out, but a loud bark in his ear stopped him. He tried to move, and he felt strong jaws clamp on his arm.

There were whistles in the air, through the dark that was now broken by the dull, diffuse light of lamps that moved through the impenetrable night, the men carrying them still shrouded in fog.

Behind him there was barking, yelping, the shouts and screams of the men he was supposed to warn as they were attacked by whatever it was that still had hold of him. Attacked and held until the police patrol could reach them and make their first successful arrest for some time.

The thing that had hold of him was the future of justice: the first police dog section in the UK.

'PC Jim' the Clifton Police Dog, described as a dog of unusual intelligence
in an article in the Western Daily Press newspaper in 1926

PART ONE 🐾
Early Days of Police Dogs

Introduction

THE POLICE DOG WE KNOW

WE ARE all familiar with the life of the police dog. We see them standing in line next to officers at riots and crowd control. We see them on television, chasing and taking down offenders. We see them as sniffer dogs sniffing out contraband.

The idea that a police dog is a natural companion to the police officer, and is by their side for the taking down of the criminal, the control of crowds, and the specialised hunt for money, drugs, and explosives is one we now take for granted.

While these may be their most high-profile roles, they are far from the only ones they have. They can help in the search for the missing and vulnerable; they can track by ground and air scent; they are used in the search for forensic traces of blood and semen; they can be trained to find dead bodies, differentiating between human and animal, as well as the recently deceased from the long since lost and buried, either by man or nature.

These are amazing, incredible animals who daily perform feats of detection, bravery, courage, intelligence and understanding that are only recognised by the public when something exceptional like the death or injury of an animal happens. It's right that these occasions are noted, but the everyday life of the police dog is equally as amazing. In this book the history of the police dog in the UK is seen through the stories of five exceptional dogs who are in some ways markers in the history and evolution of canine policing in Britain, as well as incredible personalities in their own right. The remaining story – that which starts the whole ball rolling historically – is that of four incredible canines whose presence and ability made them the standard bearers for canine crimebusting.

Police dogs are by their nature courageous, efficient, trained to a high degree, and capable of incredible feats of both bravery and intelligence. This being the case you would think that the police have used dogs for as long as there have been police forces. In fact, in the UK, the earliest example of dogs being specifically trained and used by a police force is as recent as 1908, and the organisation of dog sections as we know them now did not become a regular part of police practise until well into the 1950s.

Historical Examples

DESPITE THEIR absence from police history, dogs have always been used in some capacity or another, usually unofficially. In the Middle Ages, Parish Constables used bloodhounds for hunting down outlaws.

In more rural settings, the use of dogs to track men was akin to using dogs for hunting animals, and so these were the same dogs used were the same dogs used for everyday work. As such, the Parish Constable – appointed by the local Parish Councils allied to churches and the forerunners of the councils that would in the course of time appoint watchmen and then the local and regional police forces that we know today – would either borrow a dog, or be one of those rural workers himself, fulfilling constabulary duties alongside his daily toil.

Often, they would take their own dogs that were little more than family pets, their main use being to keep their master, the Parish Constable, company in the lonely watches of the night. In Scotland, they were using bloodhounds in much the same way and for the same reasons as by the Parish Constable.

In the cities that were starting to develop, particularly those around ports, the situation was a little different. In London, the Bow Street Runners were an organisation that preceded Sir Robert Peel's formation of what we now know as the Metropolitan Police Force.

The Bow Street Runners were a small force that worked only in the city area around the courts that gave them their name. Given their low numbers and lack of equipment and powers – fewer than the powers Peel later granted his force – the Bow Street Runners found the containment of crime difficult. So, private companies were started. These were usually funded and run by insurance companies, and worked in much the same way as early firefighters: a premium paid by the business, homeowner or landlord would see a plaque on their building which notified anyone attending of the company covering them. It was unfortunate if the first on the spot was someone employed by another company...

These companies used what were termed Nightwatchmen, and these Nightwatchmen were provided with firearms and dogs. The idea of an armed police force that is private is one that seems strange to modern readers, but the pistols, cudgels, and swords which these men would carry were more common in society than we realise.

Their dogs were, in much the same way, a violent deterrent: in the days when dogs were bred for bear baiting and dog fighting, a savage animal was not trainable and barely controllable but could attack and maim an intruder or thief with little compunction or comeback. By the time the 'Peelers' – Robert Peel's force – took to the streets, the savage dog was no longer in their armoury. Its feral nature made it hard to train and unreliable.

It's not surprising that dogs have made their way back into modern policing, as pound for pound dogs can be twice as strong as a human, the wonder is that it took so long for any organised police force to take on these intelligent animals, with their empathy for humans, and to work out how to train them.

The occasional relationship between the police and dogs continued into the late nineteenth century, where we find two examples of dogs being officially sanctioned for the first time. Neither were deemed a success.

Early Failure...

THE FIRST police dog was a fox terrier called Topper, who was based at Hyde Park Station in Central London during the 1890's. He had no handler or officer to whom he was assigned. In fact, he was made available to any officer who wished to take him out on patrol.

He was probably no more than a publicity stunt. He was adored by visitors and mentioned in many periodicals and newspapers at the time, but he wasn't trained. And without this, he was ineffective. The smarter dog can make himself useful with very little training, as Jim the Airedale terrier would prove in Bristol in the 1920s, but dogs of that quality and intelligence are few and far between, and most need the kind of training Topper was denied.

It didn't help that he was unpopular with other dogs in the street, and even less popular with policemen outside of those who handled him. Fox terriers can be difficult in their relationships with people, even if they are excellent police dogs.

There were further attempts to incorporate dogs into the Metropolitan Police Force in 1889 during the hunt for Jack the Ripper. Having drawn a blank with virtually every tool of detection at their disposal, Sir Charles Warren, who was the Commissioner of the Met at that time, sanctioned the use of bloodhounds in this case. He did this not from his own conviction, but because the press had vilified him for disdaining the use of dogs to track the killer.

He had two hounds that had been trained for what amounted to a performance for the press. They undertook a simple tracking test from one scene to another of the Ripper's crimes. It was a far from satisfactory morning's work.

Both dogs ran off, and both out of sight of the officers deputed to use them. Before bolting, one of them made matters worse by biting the Commissioner. It took a considerable search by a number of police officers before both dogs were found. Their attempts did little to endear the Met to the use of dogs, and the resulting publicity was enough to make any force think twice about canine constables.

The Right Breed?

WHEN WE think of police dogs we think mainly of three breeds. Most commonly we think of Alsatians or German Shepherds, the kind of dogs we see taking down villains and holding the line at demonstrations. In truth, they are capable of far more than this. As well as the Alsatian, the Malinois is also commonly used, a Belgian Shepherd Dog that is very similar in appearance to the Alsatian or German Shepherd.

We also tend to think of spaniels, who are usually used as

sniffer dogs. There are more breeds that can be used for sniffer duties as the ability to track is something that many dogs have. Any kind of Terrier is disposed to be an excellent dog for sniffer training, as the ability to search and find is bred into them.

Finally, we think of the bloodhound which is often used in popular fiction – particularly from the Victorian era through to the first third of the 20th century – by police or private detectives to track criminals. Sherlock Holmes is often attributed with this use, though in truth this a misremembering on a level with 'Elementary, my dear Watson' (which he never said).

However, the equally popular Sexton Blake (at his height there were four novels published every month, a weekly magazine, and stage and silent film performances dedicated to his prowess as a thief taker) always had 'the great brindled bloodhound Pedro' at his side. This cemented the bloodhound in the public imagination. Ironically, bloodhounds are actually quite poor at focused tracking as they are very hard to train and, as a result, were very rarely used.

The use of dogs in policing originated in Europe. The Parisian police began using dogs against roaming criminal gangs at night, albeit in a manner not far removed from that used by Nightwatchmen decades before in London. It was effective and opened some police minds towards the idea of using trained animals. In Prussia, also around this time, a similar use of dogs was mooted.

There had been a series of attacks on police officers made by gangs, and so a Prussian police Inspector, Franz Laufer, had the idea of using dogs to accompany his officers in order to ward off attackers. This worked: he used three dogs purchased for 500 marks each. Before purchasing, he consulted a sergeant in the force who had worked with dogs in his previous employment as a gamekeeper.

This man, Sergeant Lange, thought that the Alsatian was best suited for the task, but Laufer disagreed and thought that the Great Dane would be more intimidating to criminals.

This was partly because of the size of the dog, but also because he believed that dogs could be used not only for protecting the police but for tracking criminals from the scene of a crime. In many ways, he was ahead of the game from the rest of Europe as he had the insight to see that it was possible for a dog to fulfil more than one function. Prior to this, the idea of a dog for protection and a dog for tracking were quite separate.

In 1901, his first dog, a Great Dane called Caesar, entered service. He was muzzled at all times and always remained on a lead. Even so, he must have been quite difficult to control. This led to some scepticism about his use: would difficulty in keeping him under control prove counterproductive? Laufer stuck with his strategy, introduced more dogs, and when one of the newer dogs introduced tracked a criminal over a distance of two miles, the local police started to believe that Laufer may have a point.

While Laufer was putting his ideas into action despite his fellow officers' reluctance, over in Belgium the first organised police dog service program was being introduced, in Ghent, in 1899.

The police chief, a Mr. Van-Wesemael, was using dogs to accompany his officers on patrol at night. He used Belgian Sheepdogs, Malinois. These dogs later became much more in use as word spread about the success of the Ghent force. There is little doubt that the cooperation that Mr Van-Wesemael had from his officers contributed to the success of the project, making it the first official founding of a dog section.

The Military Mind

AFTER THE failed experiment with bloodhounds, it was widely assumed that the British police could not have much use for dogs. The ignominy of their failure and the shadow it cast over Sir Charles Warren loomed large for many Chief Constables. However, there was a lot of interest stirred up by an ardent dog trainer, Major Richardson.

A military man, he had a burning desire to get the police interested in the work being done by their counterparts on the continent, beginning with the starting of a dog section by the Met, who were his local force at that time. He was certain that if they could see the use of dogs on the continent, and look at his own training programmes, he could be of some use to them.

He was persuasive enough for the Met to send a representative to France to see some of their dogs in action. Unfortunately, the report this man came back with was not favourable: he had been unimpressed by what he witnessed and reported to the commissioner that the dogs were useful, but their expertise had been exaggerated. His conclusion was that he felt London was no place for police dogs. This was disappointing, but did not deter Major Richardson.

If the Met would not work with him, then he would turn to other forces. And here he found some who could see the potential in his theories.

There is an irony in the impetus for the use of dogs within the police coming from a military man rather than their own ranks, but then the Major was a man with an almost obsessive interest in the use of dogs. Major Edwin Heltonville Richardson was Irish by birth and came from a farming family, growing up with a lot of pets. He had worked extensively in Europe and, after retiring from the army, he started farming on the east coast of Scotland. He had a mutual interest in dog training with his wife and, in 1895, he saw someone buying a collie dog from a local Shepherd. The buyer was not a farmer and on enquiring, Richardson learned that the dog was being bought for the German army.

This sparked his interest in the possibility of training dogs for military purposes. He and his wife had already been training their dogs to work with ambulance teams. He made contact with nearby army camps, and his previous military record allowed him access to have some of the men train with his ambulance dogs.

These animals were trained to work with medical teams in remote areas, much as search and rescue dogs are used today. There were those that were so impressed that they submitted reports about the use of dogs to the war office, but no further action was taken. Undeterred, Richardson persevered with this training of dogs and relocated to the south of England, arriving at Harrow. He started to advertise his new site for the training of dogs in newspapers and attracted some press attention.

At that time, the Chief Constable of the Hertford County Constabulary was Lieutenant Colonel Henry S. Daniell. He had been aware of the use of dogs on the continent and had taken note of Richardson's training school. He recommended to his standing joint committee that they take up Major Richardson's bloodhounds and see how this worked out as a pilot programme.

On the 31st of October 1908 he published General Order 16, which said the use of Major Richardson's bloodhounds would be piloted for the detection of offenders in important cases of felony such as murder, burglary, or arson, this having been sanctioned 'as an experimental measure. All members of the force are to be especially enjoined in such cases.'

Earlier that same year in 1908, the first dog section proper in the UK was set up by the British Northeastern Railway Police. It's unthinkable that Daniell was not aware of this, and that Richardson's persistence had hit the right place and time for him to make some progress. As for Daniell, by bringing dogs into use in Hertfordshire, he paved the way for other forces who had been interested but unwilling to be the first in line. After all, if policing with dogs was to be a failure, then who would want that stigma?

Notable amongst these other forces were the Glasgow constabulary. The Glasgow criminal department had been interested in dogs after trying to trace the killer of a recently deceased criminal. Men investigating the crime had been of the opinion that a dog could have been useful in trying to find a trail for the perpetrator when little other evidence was available.

At the same time, Chief Constable James Verdia Stevenson had also been receiving complaints about the growth of violent housebreaking and other serious crimes in the area. It was at this moment that a letter from Major Richardson crossed his desk. At this point Richardson, who had been breeding now for several years, had crossbred a dog which he called the Executive, for use by the police, and had written to all Chief Constables in Britain suggesting that it could be an invaluable aid to them.

The Executive was a breed that was mainly an Airedale, with a Collie crossed for brains, and a Retriever for its sense of smell. This was Richardson's idea of an ideal police dog. The Executive was trained to assist police specifically on the night shift and, with their superior senses, locate housebreakers lying in wait in large gardens and parks. They were designed to prevent crime as much as aid in detection.

It should be noted that Major Richardson had little to do

with the setting up of the British Northeastern Railways police dogs. This came about coincidentally. At the same time Major Richardson was trying to interest police forces in his dogs, Mr. Geddes, the chief goods manager at Hull Docks in Yorkshire, visited Ghent on holiday and saw the work of the police dogs.

He was impressed with what he witnessed and, on his return, he arranged to meet with Superintendent Dobie of the North Eastern Railway police. Hull Docks were having problems with theft, and Geddes had a lightbulb moment on his holiday. Despite Richardson's crusading zeal, his real success was post-World War One, and with that continuing irony, it came from military and not police action.

When the war started, the German Armed Forces had 6,000 trained dogs. Many were trained by Inspector Laufer and Sergeant Lange, who had set up the early police dog units in Prussia. By contrast, the British Army had just one dog in service: a guard dog used by the Norfolk regiment. So it was that Richardson's dogs were initially trained for war. They were trained mainly to ignore gunfire and noise, mostly used as messenger dogs, endured awful conditions and had a short life expectancy.

Dogs who failed in action were shot like military deserters. This harsh attitude towards dogs in the military sometimes spilt over into the early days of police dogs. In many ways, these animals are still seen by some as tools and possible collateral damage rather than living beings. This attitude has changed and is still changing. There will always be some dichotomy between the theory of dog practice and the actuality when it comes to policing.

These attitudes towards the dogs, and the way in which they were treated then, seems strange and cruel to modern eyes. But it needs to be remembered that attitudes towards animal life – and towards human life – were very different in the early 1900s.

Strange as it seems, these men did have affection for their animals yet still viewed them in a different way to now. The changes in how police dogs are viewed by the force and by their handlers are in part due to those few handlers and trainers who saw the dogs as more than just another tool, like handcuffs or the truncheon (baton as it is now).

A Long And Winding Road

IF THE coming of the police dog to Britain was slow and halting, then the development of police dog sections in forces across Britain is best described as haphazard during the first third of the 20th century.

As mentioned, the first dogs introduced formally had been brought in by a section of what would later become the British Transport Police. Their success should have paved the way for a much greater action across the UK's police forces, but there was little coordination between forces at this time and the dog sections that did spring up seemed to come into being almost by accident. It took World War Two and its aftermath for the dog section to become the important factor that it is today.

The Northeastern Railway Police used their first dogs in 1908, the same year as Hertfordshire County Constabulary experimented with bloodhounds and the Glasgow Constabulary trialled the Executive. By 1910, other railway police forces were experimenting with breeds such as the Belgian Malinois, Labrador, Retriever, and German Shepherds. The use of different breeds of dog for different purposes broadened over the decades following to include Schnauzers, Akitas, Bernese Mountain Dog, Bloodhound, Border Collie, Boxer, Cane Corso, Bullmastiff, Doberman Pinscher, German Shorthair

Pointer, Rottweiler, and English Springer Spaniels. In truth, there was really no limit to the breeds that could be used. As one handler said to me: 'It doesn't matter what the dog looks like, as long as it can do the job.'

Training Days

THE TRAINING process for a dog is lengthy. It can take one to two years for the handler alone to be taught before they are even paired with a dog for operational duty. For dogs to be considered, they have to pass a basic obedience training course as they must be able to obey the commands of their handler without any hesitation.

This obedience shows that the handler has complete control. It also shows there is an empathy between handler and dog that can go beyond mere command. Dogs were initially trained with language. Commands were drummed into them as in most basic dog training. But now a lot of training is done with a ball. Ball play is very important, and one handler told me that the hunger for the ball and the desire that the dog shows for it is key to their selection. This drive is what separates a good police dog from an also-ran. The focus on the ball is a training tactic that has only been introduced in the past few decades. Before this, there was a large disparity in training methods.

Dogs are trained to be either single purpose or dual-purpose animals. The single purpose dog is one that is trained for a specific set of tasks. A sniffer dog usually has a range of search training but can sometimes be trained for just one type of search. The dual-purpose dog is used for both tracking and sniffing and deployed for use in crowd situations and for back-up to police units, is more typical.

These dogs are also referred to as general-purpose dogs. They can do almost everything a single purpose dog can do in terms of tracking, and some have the honed ability to track and sniff out explosives or narcotics. What they can't do, and what one single purpose dog trained as a sniffer can do, is track cadavers, blood or semen.

A general-purpose dog has to be very alert to the commands it is given and also learn from its handler when action is appropriate. It isn't fanciful to say that a really strong relationship between a handler and its dog can become symbiotic, with one seeming to 'read' the other.

Knowing the correct order to give a dog is crucial. A loud barking dog when in pursuit of a perpetrator is helpful and can result in them surrendering without delay.

However, a barking dog can sometimes be more of a danger to the police than a dog that stays silent. A danger also to the person it is tracking, if that person is not a perpetrator but a vulnerable and lost individual.

Tracking of this kind, where a dog's sensitivity is required, is something that a dog can do which is not often written about or recognised, but which is a valuable part of the work.

All these aspects of a police dogs' working life have evolved over the course of little more than a century.

The dogs whose stories are told here are representative of those changes, powered as much by the resourcefulness, intelligence, and courage of the animals as much as those men and women who worked with them.

In researching this book, it has become apparent to me that a truly great police dog requires an equally great handler. They have to be exceptional people to partner with such exceptional animals... right from the very beginning.

The Four Dogs Of
The Apocalypse

The Need For A Stronger Security

IN THE early years of the 20th century, the docks at Hull were a frightening place to be at night. There was no overhead light. No lamps. These were the days before electricity and fluorescent lighting. These were the days of gaslight. While this could power street lighting in the city, by the docks it was too dangerous to have any lighting. The sea and the elements could easily cause enough damage to lighting and gas piping to cause a major fire. No-one involved with the docks wanted to risk the costly loss of goods and cargo in such an accident. Especially as it was not needed for the majority of the working day.

Once night fell the docks were silent and dark. All that could be seen were large looming shapes of cargo, left dotted about almost randomly in a maze amongst which people who wished to could move unfettered and undetected. Lighting would come, but not yet.

So, for now there was a large amount of crime. It was too easy for crooks to enter the docks, to take cargo, and to leave undetected. If by any chance the police that were detailed to patrol the docks came near any criminal gangs, then it was easy for them to hide and evade those who were trying to chase them. Equally, it was also easy to ambush these policemen and put them out of action. If it was hard to steal from a dock in the dark, it was even harder to police it. The odds were in favour of the criminal, and the police fought a losing battle.

Hull Docks had been a busy port for cargo and by the same token a centre of crime for some time. However, things got worse in 1904. In this year, the Northeastern Railway, which was the main owner of the docks, applied to Parliament to build a quay along the bank of the Humber Estuary adjacent to the Albert Dock.

A year later permission was obtained and a quay was built for deep water docking, enabling larger ships with a greater amount and variety of cargo to come through. This quay was intended for shipping which carried foodstuffs and other goods which required rapid handling. The kind of goods that would attract even more crime than before.

There was a two-storey warehouse for the fruit trade on the adjacent side of Albert Dock and a single line railway swing bridge over the docks entrance was replaced with a double track bridge. There was a new passenger station for continental boat trains also. The quay's support was formed on Blue Gum and Pitch Pine Timber pylons. It was equipped with a hydraulically powered capstan for shunting and electric cranes.

A water supply to service ships and any equipment for fire fighting was fitted along with gas lighting. New designs, ensuring greater safety, were used. This was the first time that lighting had been available on the docks for any usage after dark, but its use was still mostly for workers and passengers in those twilight hours around dawn and dusk. Come night, the area around the quay was dark and silent still. As the docks became busier and the new quay attracted more trade, more cargo, and more goods, so perversely it attracted more criminals.

Homeless people would also shelter in the docks, finding in the newer buildings some relief from the weather and the cold. This was a problem for the police as they would steal from the crates in order to eat, in order to find clothing, in order to find shelter. The dock had always attracted some homeless and some crime, however this increased dramatically following the success of the new works.

All of this presented a growing problem for the Northeastern Railway Police. As with all ports and docks, the local constabulary did not find these areas under their jurisdiction. Instead, they were the purview of the police forces run by the railways whose main trade lay in the goods they transported to and from the dock. It was, after all, less than a century since Stevenson's Rocket, one of the first steam locomotives, and the birth of the rail system. Passengers were not the primary concern of the rail companies at this time. Their profit lay in the trade they transported and had taken over from the waterways.

The Northeastern Railway police needed to work out how they could deal with the new influx of homelessness and the rise in crime affecting their trade. Quickly. Previous police patrols had been intermittently effective, but were constrained by the need to work on foot amongst the cargo crates, and to keep their presence hidden by the dark. They needed something that would enable them to move swiftly and sure footed in the black of the night-time dock.

Their solution came about by chance, and was not to be found close to home, but overseas.

While the Northeastern Railway police were working on their own plans, the chief general goods manager for the whole of Hull Docks, Mr Geddes, was taking his vacation in Belgium. As part of his journey, he was in Ghent. It wasn't a planned visit, but it was a fortuitous one as while he was there, he chanced to see some of Ghent's police dogs in action. He was impressed by what he saw, and it got him thinking.

On his return to Hull, he arranged a meeting with Superintendent J. Dobie, who had been given the responsibility of policing the docks at Hull. Dobie had been facing an increasing raft of problems as the growth of the docks and the incrementally increasing issues with crime and the homeless were giving him a headache of trying to cover more ground with the same amount of manpower as before. So, it was with some interest that he spoke with Mr Geddes.

'I saw something while I was in Ghent that might be a solution to our problems...'

Geddes outlined what he had seen when in Belgium. Dobie had been aware of some of the false starts that had been made, but he was not convinced.

'I've heard about these dogs, but there's no real evidence that they're effective. If I spend money, bring them in, and it falls flat, then it's my job on the line.'

Geddes was adamant. 'What I saw was amazing. With the right training, this could be just what we're looking for here. We have to try it.'

'I have to try it...' Dobie fell silent, thinking about the pressure he had been under. He understood that this was an option that could help him police the docks with greater effect. If it worked. Even if it didn't work, an initial experiment could be made which would not cost his bosses a large amount, and he could easily return to what he saw as more conventional methods. After all, it was not entirely his idea. He said: 'You know it'll be a problem for you as well. If it falls flat, I mean.'

Geddes leaned across the desk. 'I don't think it will. I think it's the future...'

So, in November 1907 Geddes, Dobie and some other officers

travelled to Ghent on a fact-finding mission. There they saw the dog section, which at that time numbered some 40 officers and dogs. Impressed by what he saw in person, Dobie now believed that a similar scheme set up to service Hull Docks would be of benefit to him.

On returning to Hull, Dobie called Inspector Dobson into his office and charged him with the responsibility of setting up this new section. He put a pile of notes before him. 'Read that, and tell me what we need to make this work here.'

Dobson studied Dobie's findings, and decided that the kind of dog Dobie recommended would be all wrong for the docks. Dobie had been so impressed by the section in Ghent that he was set on following their lead and using Malinois as the breed of dog to be trained. Dobson could not agree with this. One of the reasons he had been chosen was because he was a dog man, and he knew his breeds and the kind of activities that they had been bred for. A Malinois was an excellent town and country dog, but the environment of the dock had different requirements.

Dobson decided to use Airedale Terriers. As a breed, they were a new strain of terrier, having initially been bred just 30 years earlier. The first registered Airedale was in 1876. As with all terriers, they were hunting dogs, bred to sniff out and eliminate vermin.

The Airedale was bred for the specific purpose of hunting vermin down by rivers, which made them perfect for use in a dock environment, where the water and the clutter of packing cases and crates made for a territory not far removed from the banks and gullies along a river. They were not as large as Malinois, but they were not small dogs either. They were large enough and sturdy enough to be able to carry their weight if required to engage physically with a target.

Allied to this was their essential terrier characteristics: they were stronger and hardier dogs for a dock than the Malinois and they had a keener sense of smell, which would be invaluable as they would be working in poor light.

Another large consideration and advantage in Dobson's view was that the Airedale had a thick, wiry coat. This would help keep them warm and offer some padding and protection. More importantly, their coat was less likely than that of other dogs to pick up mud from the docks, and so they would require less grooming. The less grooming the dog required, the more time it could spend in service, so the more time the handler could spend training with it.

And so it was that early in 1908 the first police dogs to be used in the UK began their patrol at Hull docks. There were four of them: Jim Vic, Mick, and Ben. (Ben is sometimes referred to as Whisk – it's generally agreed that he was named Ben, and Whisk is possibly the result of an error in some reporting). They were used only at night and they would patrol with their handlers. They were trained specifically to protect the police uniform.

In fact, such was their training that when their handlers were out of uniform, the dogs would growl and act hostile towards them. Jim's handler was reported to be Sergeant Allinson. However, while he was certainly one of the handlers, other reports suggest that the dogs had no individual handler, and the men deputed to the dog section handled the four dogs as a group, with the dogs responding to any one of them.

These were early days, and at this point the advantages that a unique relationship between one handler and one dog, as we can see from much of the history, had not yet been identified. It was an omission that continued for a few decades after this.

There was a lot of press coverage in the Yorkshire area

regarding the new dog section. One such report read: 'In a novel experiment by the Northeastern Railway police, dogs are used as detectives on the docks at Hull. They consist of a number of trained Airedale Terriers which in company with the railway police patrol throughout the night and capture thieves, tramps, and other persons who may be sleeping out. The dogs are trained to obey a police whistle, and to chase and stop a man who is running away.'

Not much training required, and no complex instruction or difficult tasks for the dogs to master. Yet this is still a giant leap from letting loose a bloodhound and hoping for the best, as Charles Warren had with the Met, or having a dog merely as company at night.

The question was: would they be effective? Would Dobie's experiment work?

Crime On The Run

THE DOGS were extremely successful. Imagine: it's a dark night. The police can't use lamps, they can't use torches as this would give away their presence. They're hunting for thieves, they're hunting for the homeless who would wreck the cargo. It's a world of shadows every night, and this was what they had felt they were chasing. The dogs they have just been given are sent on ahead of them. It's cold. It's foggy. The only thing that can penetrate this murk is the sound of the whistle from the handler.

It's terrible weather if you're a man: the police and the thieves are both working at a disadvantage. Not so much for Vic, Jim, Mick, and Ben: bred to hunt along rivers and streams by day or night, the cold doesn't penetrate their thick coats, the murk and gloom doesn't get in the way of their noses. Smell doesn't need light. They follow a trail, not a path. They are used to dodging in and out of obstacles and keeping their feet on the most treacherous of surfaces. It's an ability bred into them from their forebears and honed by training and practice.

It doesn't take the dogs long to locate an intruder. They raise the alarm by barking. Their handlers follow. In the dark it's difficult to see what's going on. Shadows obscure everything. Out of these shadows comes substance as the police run into the thieves, interrupted in their task.

There is a fight. In this fight, it's hard for the police to see who are the enemy and who are their allies. There is no light by which they can tell who is friend or who is foe. But the dogs can tell. Because they've been able to track by smell, they can differentiate between the two. They can grab and detain the thieves, the homeless, those who should not be there. They clear up the docks and make them safe again at night. At least for a while…

Sadly, there is little record of the careers and the lives of these four dogs. There are a few photographs, particularly of Jim and Sergeant Allinson, and these show that the four dogs were not uniform. One of them had light coloured fur, another seemed to be tan, while the remaining two were dark. No-one bothered to record which dog was which.

To treat the four of them as one seems to do them an injustice given their pioneer status, and yet it was together that they lived and worked, and together that they had their status and power. They worked as a team, and so that is how they should be remembered.

Their training was basic and geared towards search and find on a simplistic level. The men handling them were also starting from a point of knowing nothing other than what they had gleaned from Dobson, and from Dobie and his visit to Ghent. In truth, they started – dog and man – from the point of view that there was a specific job to be done, and on the docks this was all they needed to know.

Back at the turn of the 20th century, dogs in service were not treated as anything other than tools: this is not to say that the handlers did not have affection for the four dogs; after all, the affinity between dogs and their human companions is what made the idea of using them so appealing and practical in the first instance. Whatever else is known or not known, and for all the speculation about their lives, their status as the first working police dogs in the UK can never be taken away from them.

And let's be honest, if you were a gambler, would you bet on a man who could not see in the darkness and needed to remain on two feet in treacherous circumstances, or on a tough little terrier with a strong jaw, sharp teeth, a keen sense of smell that defied the dark, and the surefootedness bred into him? I know where my money would go…

A First Hand Account

MOST PRESS reports of the time are brief, and if you can find them in century-old newspapers and magazines they offer you very little in detail – which makes the following report all the more vital. It appeared in, of all places, the *Dundee Evening Telegraph* of Friday, 29th July 1910.

RAILWAY POLICE DOGS ARE TERRORS TO EVIL DOERS.

MOST docks, particularly those belonging to private corporations, are protected by unscalable walls, but Hull docks differ with others in this respect, as they are not fenced in any way and are consequently open to the depredations of thieves and the unenviable attention of tramps and others. As an additional protection to these docks, a scheme has been formulated by which the police constables of the North-Eastern Railway on night duty will be assisted by dogs.

The dogs, which are Airedale terriers, are so brave that they will attack a man even though he is armed with a revolver or a club. On duty the dogs are muzzled, as otherwise they would tear any tramp to pieces.

An officer at three o'clock one morning was passing along the quayside, says a writer in the Railway and Travel Monthly, when suddenly his dog, a favourite named Whisk, flew to a large hamper which was standing alongside several more. The dog jumped on the top of the hamper, and a voice said, "Oh my head." The owner of the voice proved to be a rough-looking navvy, who said he had walked all the way from Leeds the other day. Rough-looking fellow as he was, he was grateful when he was given his liberty.

On another occasion an officer with his dog was passing a railway carriage when his canine companion commenced to growl and jump around him. On investigation two men were found inside the carriage. One of the best and keenest dogs in the Hull kennels is " Jim," and it was this splendid animal that was responsible for the arrest of two notorious thieves who were plundering a coffee house.

This fascinating snapshot of the dogs in action mentions Jim by name. The best and keenest, indeed. There is something about the name Jim when attached to a police dog... It also mentions a dog called Whisk, and this report may be where the misnaming of one of the first four dogs originates.

This was two years after the scheme had first been put into operation, and more dogs had been added to the kennels in Hull Docks. Whisk was obviously a later addition to the kennels, and in trying to glean more information about the first dogs, this report has probably been misinterpreted. It clears up one mystery, but leaves you wanting more.

A Growing Success

SOON AFTER the initial scheme was put into operation, in November 1908, it was extended to Hartlepool Docks. Shortly after that, it went to the Tyne Dock, and the Middlesbrough Dock, all of these being policed by the Northeastern Railway police. For something like this to develop within a span of less than 12 months is a testament to the achievements of those first four dogs.

So it was that the pattern of each new section followed the initial section at Hull. The dogs were all trained at home, but kennels were erected at the docks police station. Although the trainers were also handlers, they did not at this point retain their dog: the 'pool' of dogs and handlers remained as at Hull. There was a kennelman allotted to the kennels and he was usually a Constable who had been a gamekeeper before joining the force.

Many of the forces outside major cities had men who had been gamekeepers join up as the major estates started to cut back on workers. And not just in England, as Sergeant Lange, right hand man to Inspector Lauffer the Prussian dog pioneer, had also been a gamekeeper at one time. Used to working dogs as a part of their job, these men were obvious choices to work in the new dog sections.

At these kennels each dog had his own individual space with a run, and they were also issued with a thick coat to wear during bad weather. Of course, as a terrier trained to suit outdoor life, issuing a thick coat for bad weather may seem strange: a cold night on the river bank hunting vermin is just the same as a foggy night on the Tyne Dock hunting a different kind of prey, after all. But the coat was not just useful for the weather, being thick and padded it protected the dog not only from the cold, but from any blows that may be aimed at it by its enemies in the course of duty.

The dogs were only used at night. They were trained with treats to protect the police uniform. This was added to the previous training to attack anyone who was not wearing a uniform. This was the police taking no chances. There was little possibility of any innocent bystander being attacked in error, as anyone who would venture on to the dock at night was only there for one purpose, and could be considered a suspect. Once business had closed for the day, any workers were long gone. The only people who would have any business prowling the docks in the darkness would be potential criminals.

Following this extension in the use of dogs, the Ghent police sent Commissioner Piron over to visit the new dog sections and he was delighted at the thief-taking these dogs could accomplish. He was not the only one impressed. Less than two years later, in early 1910, the *Northeastern Railway magazine* gave an account of an early arrest by the dogs:

'In the early hours of the morning, a policeman accompanied by a dog was patrolling Saint Andrews Dock in Hull and seeing a man loitering in a suspicious manner called upon him to stop. The man took no notice. So, the officer slipped his dog.

One of the best, it soon had the man down and begging for mercy. Having secured this man, the officer made a search and found the window of a refreshment room broken. He entered and called upon those inside to surrender. Receiving no response, he called out that he had taken his dog's muzzle off and immediately came the reply. 'Put his muzzle back on sir, and we will come out.' With which two burly fellows came from behind the counter. They, along with their companion, were marched by the officer and his dog to the police station, a distance of about half a mile, without the slightest resistance. They turned out to be notorious burglars and received their just desserts.'

The Growth Of Dog Sections For The Railway Police

THE SUCCESS of the pioneering Northeastern Railway police scheme meant that police dogs from Hull were sent to other railway companies and police forces around the country. The first of these dogs was Charlie, who was used by the nearby Hull and Barnsley Railway police.

In 1912, he was on patrol with his handler PC Easton when they came across a man armed with a knife. The officer's attempt to arrest the man resulted in him being stabbed in the chest. It was fortunate that he had a thick great coat on which prevented the blade from penetrating too far. Charlie jumped on the man to defend his master and held him down until he could be arrested.

As a result of this Charlie, along with PC Easton, was invited to Crufts in London, the following year. He was awarded a shield and medal by the Canine Defence League and became the first police dog to receive such an award.

The good work of the police dogs became known to the military, and during the early months of World War One, 10 police dogs from the Hull Docks dog section were conscripted into the army to accompany the 17th Northumberland Fusiliers, which was the Northeastern Railway Pioneer Battalion. These dogs were used as guard dogs in France.

The irony, of course, is that it was Army man Lieutenant

Colonel Richardson who had initially begun to promote the use of police dogs with his own attempts to persuade the Met police some eight years earlier, in 1906. Richardson's continued work after the Great War was no doubt spurred on by seeing this justification of his early efforts.

Further irony lay in the fact that the later use of Alsatians in the police also stems from the Great War. Whilst it was Airedales that were used by the British army, taken from the Northeastern Railway police, their own dog section later reviewed its own practises in and the trainers in Hull decided that they would switch to Alsatians as these dogs had been seen in action for the enemy by dog handlers during the Great War.

Their effective use by the German army, and their efficiency and excellence at their tasks had been noted. So, again, it is thanks to the military – in a roundabout fashion – that we owe the use of Alsatians in the British police forces.

Business As Usual

THE GREAT WAR disrupted life in the UK as it did across Europe, but of course it had to be business as usual in the docks, or at least as close to this as was possible. The continued supply chain of cargo ships from across the globe needed to be maintained. The large numbers of men conscripted or volunteering for the services put strain on police forces across the country. Being a policeman was a protected occupation and there was no conscription for these, but this would not prevent some officers from volunteering regardless.

Fewer police officers could have meant more opportunity for crime. They were deprived of their dogs as well as their men, but the business of crime prevention continued regardless. And it was just as successful. The dog section at Hull continued to be led by Inspector Dobson. By 1918, no less than 185 suspects had been detained at the docks, the majority with the assistance of these dogs. Over the four years of the Great War, that averages at just under one arrest per week. That may not sound like much, but with the increased efficiency granted by use of dogs, it speaks of how the opportunity for dock raids had been reduced as much as the thief-taking capabilities of the section.

The British Transport Police, as they are now known, are proud of their role as the pioneers of police dog use in this country, and rightly so. Initially, they were comprised of a number of disparate and separated forces who patrolled the railways and the docks. These forces were usually allied to either the dock authorities or the railway companies who operated in those regions.

It was only after the review in 1923 by the Hull section dog trainers that the many railway and dock police forces decided their best course of action would be to amalgamate. It was at this time that they became the British Transport Commission Police, later dropping the 'Commission' to become known as the British Transport Police, or BTP.

By combining their resources, they became the second largest police force in the country. At this time, they had 24 police dogs. A new training centre was established at Inman's Farm, Hedon Hall, near Hull. The officer placed in charge of this establishment was Inspector John Morrell. Under his stewardship, the dog section was soon increased to 75 dogs. Morrell continued for over three decades. It was only on his death, in 1960, that he was succeeded by Inspector Herbert Shelton, who was recruited from another force to fulfil a role that Morrell had not only made his own, but which had shaped the way in which police forces looked at dogs.

The Slow Spread Of The Police Dog

THE PIONEERING work of the British Transport Police took some time to filter through to the police at large. As we have seen, other forces had made some tentative starts on the use of dogs. Surrey began their initial experiments just after the Great War, while Hertfordshire, spurred on by their contact with Lieutenant Colonel Richardson, had begun their initial use in 1908, albeit in nowhere near as organised a fashion as Dobie and Dobson in Hull.

Glasgow, also following in the footsteps of Richardson and using his Executive breed, had started theirs in 1910. However, it was not until the 1930s that many forces started to look at the use of dogs with any degree of seriousness. In fact, in 1934 the Home Office set up a committee to evaluate the use of dogs within the police service. Initially, they felt that dogs on the streets would harm the police in public relations.

There was an idea that the public would feel that the police did not consider themselves safe on the street without help; this being so, how could the public then feel safe? The reaction when dogs were commonly used, some two decades later, gave lie to that although it does make you wonder what kind of research was conducted to come to such an odd conclusion.

Despite these findings, the following year, His Majesty's Inspector of Constabulary agreed that the Met could have two Labradors, which commenced patrol in 1938 on the streets of Brixton and Southwark.

This was exactly 30 years after the first dogs had been used by the railway police. It's astounding in retrospect that the success of the BTP had been so roundly ignored by other forces – and the Home Office – for so long. The dogs were both black

Labradors, handsome looking animals who were given unacceptable names we won't repeat.

At the outbreak of World War Two, the two Labradors were transferred to the Cheshire Constabulary, and it was not until after the war that the training schools at Imber Court and then Keston were set up by the Met police. Many forces did not take the idea of dogs seriously. Their attitude was still rooted in those early years of the dog being nothing more than an accompaniment to the Watchman and not a trained and useful police operative in their own right.

Given that Surrey and the Met were the two that took the idea of dogs with a more serious intent and purpose than most forces, and that Hertfordshire and Glasgow picked up the baton and then dropped it, we're going to be looking at the histories of these four forces in brief, seeing as they found themselves as – sometimes unwilling-- pioneers.

Surrey

THE COUNTY Constabulary first started using police dogs during the Great War. There was a prisoner of war camp established at Firth Hill, Frimley. Most of the inmates were quite happy to sit out the war, but occasionally some felt they should try and escape.

The surrounding countryside was ideal cover for this. It was a distraction for the local police, and not one that they relished. The country was densely wooded in places, and it took a lot of man hours that needed to be deployed elsewhere in order to look for escaped POWs who had nowhere to run. To assist in searching for them, police at Camberley obtained three bloodhounds for the purpose of tracking. These were kennelled at Camberley Police Station and handled by a Sergeant Kenwood and his assistant, PC Pink. They were used many times with success but their use was discontinued after the war as there were few duties for them that headquarters could think of at this point.

It wasn't until 1933, shortly before the Home Office report, that the head of CID, Inspector Tom Roberts, persuaded the Chief Constable to allow a PC Potter, who was stationed at Ash, between Canterbury and Sandwich, to use the blood-hounds that he kept for himself in selective police work.

Roberts felt that it might be worth trialling their use as Potter, a bloodhound breeder and enthusiast in his outside work, had them in situ. Roberts' scheme was for Potter to have a five-year trial with the dogs, not just in Surrey but also in Hampshire and Buckinghamshire if they requested them.

Given that bloodhounds generally do not live up to their name or reputation, Potter showed that he was a born dog trainer as his hounds proved themselves particularly success-ful when requested to find evidential clues at crime scenes, retrieve discarded stolen property, and track missing persons. It is fascinating to speculate if Potter's success with his hounds could be duplicated with other bloodhounds, as it may have changed the development of the police dog – particularly spe-cialist sniffer dogs – as we know them. Unfortunately, the five years were up just before the outbreak of World War Two, and as with so many things this programme was not continued in the face of more pressing matters.

In a time when the idea of using dogs for police work was widely unaccepted, why was Tom Roberts so keen on blood-hounds, and why was Potter the man of his choice?

Earlier in his career, when he was Detective Sergeant, Roberts had been called to the scene of a shop break-in that had occurred on the border of Surrey and West Sussex. The

West Sussex force had been experimenting with bloodhounds and had one on the scene. It took its handler to a railway track, and proceeded along for some distance before losing the scent. The West Sussex officers at the scene were dismissive, and made their opinion of dogs clear. It was no wonder that their force soon discontinued dog use until after World War Two.

Tom Roberts, however, was not so sure. He had followed the handler along the track and, as he went, he noticed a heel print which was from a shoe that was fairly common at the time. Something nagged at him and when he returned to the police station, he checked up and found that there had been more than 20 break-ins which had occurred in isolated villages, but all close to a rail line. He suggested that a watch be kept on those areas along the line that had not been subject to a break-in.

It was a good hunch: the first night a watch was kept, the thief was apprehended. And as it happens, the arresting officer was PC Potter, whose bloodhound gave the alert. Potter had brought the dog with him for company in the watches of the night.

Roberts, of course, associated Potter with the dogs when he formulated his idea. He gave the West Sussex dog the credit for his inspiration, but was also shrewd enough to note that this was a combination of dog and deduction. The notion that a dog could solve a crime all by itself might be feasible on occasion, but was unrealistic as a 100 percent expectation. He was a man ahead of his time. That would benefit Surrey in the years to come, as would recruitment from the Met of the man who changed the course of police dog training.

Surrey, as a County force, later went on to become the leader in its development of police dogs, and was instrumental in setting up dog sections in other parts of the world, such as Kenya 1949, New Zealand in 1956, Uganda in 1964, and Barbados in 1980.

Hertfordshire

THE HERTFORDSHIRE force's interest in dogs was spurred on by contact with Major, later Lieutenant Colonel Richardson. Lieutenant Colonel Henry Daniell, Chief Constable of Hertfordshire, also had a military background. This was not in itself unusual for Chief Constables and Commissioners, who tended not to be police lifers, but drafted in from the outside.

It may have made him more sympathetic to Richardson's concerns, along with the continuing reports of Richardson's trips to Paris where he would try to persuade the Parisien gendarmerie to adopt his bloodhounds for use, that caught Daniell's eye. It was these press articles that persuaded him to adopt the motions at the annual standing committee of the County Constabulary which led to Hertfordshire retaining the use of Richardson's bloodhounds... if such an occasion for their use should arise.

Daniell was hedging his bets. 'If' meant that Richardson would have to kennel and pay for his dogs, not sell them to Hertfordshire or charge for their keep; and it was bloodhounds they required, not the new Executive breed Richardson was developing.

This new breed would be a general purpose dog, to be used much as Hull used their Airedales. Daniell wanted the use of dogs purely as trackers, not wishing to risk injury to the public and the embarrassing questions that would follow.

News of Hertfordshire's adoption of the bloodhound spread. It was not long after this, in 1911, that the Chief Constable of Liverpool also ordered a number of dogs from Major Richardson's Harrow kennels. These hounds were to accompany police in six outlying districts of Liverpool on night duty. Their use was not clearly defined: as bloodhounds, they were thought of primarily as trackers, and yet they were being used as a general purpose dog, and only at night. Again, the echoes of the Nightwatch and their companion dogs were hard to ignore.

While Liverpool were happy to buy dogs from Richardson, the Hertfordshire County Constabulary seemed unwilling to actually purchase dogs from Richardson. While still keeping their hiring agreement in place, they decided to see if it was possible to train their own. Around the time that Liverpool were taking the plunge, Daniell issued General Order Number Seven, which stated that the Chief Constable would offer prizes of three pounds, two pounds and one pound for dogs which, in the opinion of a duly appointed judge, were 'most suitable and best trained for the purposes of police protection'.

Amongst the dogs considered in this competition were Old English Sheepdogs, Collies, Airedales, Retrievers, and the large Irish Terrier. It was an initiative that came to very little in the end: Daniell had a definite interest in the use of dogs, but seemed undecided on how best to proceed, stunting the development of dog use in Hertfordshire for another few years.

Glasgow

WHILE HERTFORDSHIRE blew hot and cold, unsure of how best to utilise the dog in police work, Glasgow had little hesitation, and decided to dive straight into the use of dogs. Unfortunately, they also had little idea of how best to use their newly acquired dogs. Perhaps this was because Chief Constable James Verdier Stevenson was coming under pressure from his bosses following an epidemic of crime in the city, much of which affected the emergent middle classes; housebreaking was rife in the newly-affluent areas of the city, and these outraged homeowners were the up and coming councillors who controlled the police purse strings.

Many of the break-ins were not just burglaries, but involved violence against householders who did not co-operate. In the poorer areas, there was an increase in violent crimes and assault. It seemed there was a crime wave set to sweep away the Chief Constable if he did nothing to stem the tides.

It was fortuitous, then, that in February 1910, Stevenson received a letter from Richardson which put forward the case for a police force to make use of his new Executive breed. Richardson was summoned to police headquarters, in Glasgow's St Andrews Square, where he presented his theories and evidence of the Executive's suitability as a working dog. Richardson was convinced that his new breed was the answer to any Constabulary's requirements.

Richardson's letter had also appeared in the *Glasgow Herald*, and this helped with Stevenson's case when he brought the matter before the Watching and Lighting Committee, whose budget the police came under. He needed all the help he could get.

According to records, one councillor, Roderick Scott, expressed his disapproval of the scheme by stating 'why should the police have dogs as if they were living in Borneo or some of these savage countries?'... Perhaps Mr Scott had missed press reports of one householder, a Mr Fleming, who had been cleared of murder for shooting a violent burglar, John McLeod, who had threatened him with a 10-inch knife during a break-in. Glasgow was obviously pretty savage at this point in time. The same could be said of another councillor who stated, when Stevenson told him that dogs were used by the Paris Police, that Glasgow was fortunate that it had 'no hooligans of the Parisian type'...

Given this level of argument, it was amazing that the committee eventually voted in favour of trialling dogs and so purchased four Executives from Richardson at a cost of £21. Richardson trained his dogs to assist officers on night shift, and with their superior senses to locate housebreakers who may be lying in wait in the large gardens and parks that were a hallmark of the middle-class areas being hit by the crime wave.

As an aside, it can be seen here how Richardson was keen to tailor the training of his dogs to the demands of a specific purchasing Constabulary. It does beg the question that if the Chief Constables of the United Kingdom had been more open minded when approached by Richardson, would the development of police dogs in the service have been much quicker, and perhaps a smoother transition?

Perhaps not. Once the dogs had left Richardson's kennels, they could only do their best, and were reliant on an equal capability from their handlers. And at this point, the men were far, far behind the dogs in knowing what they should be doing.

The first two dogs arrived in June 1910. They were kennelled at the Central Police Office, Turnbull Street, Glasgow before being posted to F, or Maryhill Division, serving Kelvinside. There is a photograph of one of these dogs with the officer charged with them when they arrived, Sergeant Robert Glenn, the Bar Officer at Central Police Office.

From this, it is clear to see that despite the Retriever and Collie that was part of the breed, the Executive is almost identical to an Airedale, being of the same size and with the same skull shape. It had the same length of leg, the same thick wiry coat, and perhaps the only thing that sets it apart is that the muzzle is a little less terrier-sharp, with a broader look akin to a Retriever or Labrador.

It proved itself as fiercely brave, loyal, and protective of its handler. As did all four dogs, for the second pair of dogs arrived in Glasgow on June 29th. These two were to be used in the Pollokshields area, which was the G, or Queens Park Division.

The dogs and the handlers allotted to them took short training courses before they were sent to the areas concerned. The names of the dogs, unfortunately, were not recorded apart from one, which we know was called Bob. Like Jim, this seemed to be a good name for an Airedale or Airedale-related dog at the time.

The dogs were noted to be strong in build, good natured and obedient, and indifferent to cold and exposure. All, of course, the reasons why Hull had chosen Mick, Jim, Vic and Ben a couple of years before. There was extensive coverage in the newspapers for the arrival of the four dogs, although the Chief Constable, oddly, chose to omit any mention of them in his annual report for 1910.

The *Glasgow Herald*, however, following on from its printing of Richardson's letter, which started this ball rolling, stated, 'This is the first time that dogs have been utilised in Great Britain as an aide to the police, but their use abroad is not uncommon.' Of course, as we have seen this was not an accurate statement, but it does reflect the lack of knowledge within the general public and also the press about developments elsewhere in the British Isles. Once again, it seems as though the achievements of the railway police existed only in the shadows.

There are scant records of any police use of dogs in Glasgow, and those available only really stem from 1953, when there was an official formation of the City of Glasgow Police Dog Branch. This is just a further demonstration of the haphazard nature in which police dogs were taken up around the country, and the way in which their adoption for use was treated.

However, we can assume that the experiment with the initial four dogs was a success, as there is an article from the *Glasgow Evening Times* of 3rd February 1913, which confirms that there was a continued dog presence.

Although it has to be said that this report is not the kind of thing of which Richardson would have approved. It tells of an unarmed Constable who opened a Suburban Police Box but did not see that a dog had been left inside, unmuzzled. The dog bit the constable's leg. It was enough to send him off duty, although not a serious wound. So certainly, the dogs were still around three years after the initial purchase, if perhaps not as well trained as they should have been. It can't have been one of the Executives, surely: Richardson trained them too well for such an act.

The Influence Of Jim, Vic, Mick and Ben

ALTHOUGH WE know little about these four pioneer dogs, their legacy and testament to their dedication to duty lay in the fact that the dog section at Hull grew, and led to other railway police forces taking up the baton. From there, the BTP led the way in developing police dog training and use. Other forces looked to them, learned from them, and built on their knowledge and experience.

Now, we have dedicated dog sections in all forces, and breeding programmes to provide dogs that are designed to succeed. Of course, it wasn't always that way, and some forces were slower than others in developing.

In Bristol, despite having a thriving port which had its own need of a railway police dog section, the local Bristol police were slow in adopting the idea of a police dog. What they did not realise as the 1920s dawned was that they would have a police dog whether they liked it or not, as one remarkable dog – yet another Airedale, and yet another Jim – decided that he wanted to join the local police.

Jim: A Police Dog's Vocation

A Foundling Who Found Himself

IF YOU went back over a 100 years ago, you wouldn't recognise Bristol as it was then. Like most ports around the UK, it was a target for bombers during World War Two and although the Blitz in London and the decimation of Liverpool are more widely known, it would be wrong to think that Bristol was left relatively unscathed.

The city centre was flattened by bombing, with streets that had been unchanged since the 1700s wiped out in just a few nights. Streets that had been teeming with life were now just lines in the rubble. From this, the city was built anew, and so anyone born after 1950 could have no idea what it was like to live in those tightly packed streets with their ancient houses.

The dog that this chapter centres around was born into that old city and the coppers he chose to spend his life with walked streets that exist now only in the imagination and old photographs. It was truly a different world and you have to take yourself back there in order to understand why this dog was so remarkable both in his character and in his actions.

If you look at the docks that were patrolled by Jim, Mick, Vic and Ben, you will notice that the area is made up of historic, unchanged structures alongside newer builds. Although both

Hull and Cardiff were also bombed, neither suffered quite the same damage as Bristol, which saw much of its history erased.

Two decades before the desolation, when this story takes place, Bristol was a tight-knit community, living and working cheek by jowl in a city clustered around its docks. There were very few phones in the residential areas of the city, and the pace of life was lagging behind the larger cities of the UK. There was still plenty of crime: where there is a port with people coming and going from land and sea, there will always be the chance to make illicit gains. However, this criminal activity was centred around the docks area, and in areas like Kings Square and Brandon Hill, it was much quieter.

The city was policed by the Bristol force, now part of the Avon and Somerset Police Force but then an independent body. The idea of dogs being used by the local coppers was not something that had crossed anyone's mind.

It took a dog making its own decisions to become the first police dog in Bristol to change this. A decisive and remarkable animal with a character larger than life. His incredible story has been preserved in part by Alan Vowels, resident historian of the Avon and Somerset Police Force. And remarkably, given the destruction that happened in the years after this took place, the two main landmarks in this story can still be seen today.

A Fortuitous Discovery

KINGS SQUARE was built in 1755 and, as its name suggests, is a square which serves as an enclosed garden for the Georgian Houses which surround it. Like the terraces and squares of Bath, these were built at a time when the wool and corn merchants of the West Country were making their fortunes, and although the buildings in Bristol have suffered in changing times, the houses and the Square itself have remained untouched. The gardens were originally planted with cross rows of lime trees to form avenues along the paths in and around the Square. By the 1920s, these trees had long since been uprooted and replaced by more modest trees and shrubs. Those that had formed a boundary wall around the Square had also gone and were now replaced by less ornate but more practical iron railings.

The Square was a quiet place, used mostly by people who wished to stop and while away a few minutes in relative solitude, but was also a quick shortcut across if you happened to be in a hurry. Which is exactly what it was for Father O'Connell on a summer's day in 1922. A Parish Priest is always busy, always has places to be, and so he bustled through the Square with no time for stopping and smelling the roses… or any other flower amongst those that were in bloom.

But something did stop him, unexpectedly. From the corner of his eye, he could see an object in one of the bushes that shouldn't have been there. It was a cardboard box. Who, he wondered, would just dump a box in a place like this? And then he realised what it was that had made him pause: the box was moving. There was something alive inside there.

Father O'Connell turned around and, in doing so, ensured the saving of a man's life some years in the future.

He made his way over to the box and examined it. Cautiously, he lifted the lid to take a look inside, and was met with the face of a tiny ball of black and brown fluff that looked up at him. Who on earth could be so heartless as to dump such a creature, he wondered. He lifted the puppy out of the box and examined it. It stared at him imploringly as it wriggled. It was almost as if it were asking him to rescue it with its big, brown eyes.

Of course he was going to rescue it – he wasn't even sure what kind of a dog it was as he was no expert – but what he was actually going to do with it was another matter. He didn't want a dog himself, did not have the time to devote to it, but he couldn't leave it. He made a snap decision. He was on his way to St Mary's Private Hospital when he found the little feller, so why not present it to the nuns who ran the hospital? If they didn't want it, they'd be sure to know someone who did.

Father O'Connell scooped up the box and the puppy and carried on to the hospital, where he was greeted by a puzzled Mother Superior, asking him why he was carrying a dog. When he explained, she took the brown and black bundle and examined it.

Like everyone who would meet the dog in later years, she could see the intelligence in his eyes, and immediately made a decision. She told the Priest that the Sisters would be only too glad to take the pup in and look after him. The Hospital could do with a resident dog. It would be good for the patients to see him about the place, and he would also be useful if there were any rats.

The Priest looked at her quizzically.

'Do you not know what kind of a dog this is?' she asked him. 'Have you never seen an Airedale before?'

Father O'Connell shrugged, 'A dog is a dog to me. I have no idea about them.'

So, the Mother Superior patiently explained that Airedales, like most terriers, were born ratters and hunters of vermin. Surely, he had noticed the number of terriers around the docks? Again, he shrugged, 'I'll just have to take your word for it...'

And so it was settled. The puppy would be a hospital dog.

The dog himself, on the other hand, would have other ideas.

Named, And Given A Good Upbringing

THE SISTERS were excited about having a dog to look after, and they gladly paid the licensing fee necessary in the days when all dogs had to have a licence, paid yearly. The notion of nuns spoiling and lavishing affection on a puppy may sound unusual, but they took to him with love, and he had a very good year growing up and having the run of the hospital buildings and grounds. St Mary's Hospital was – and is, although it is now converted to apartments – a large Italianate building that forms a square of its own, with a garden and grounds in the centre and an entrance lodge at the gates that exit onto the main road.

The Sisters named the dog Jim, and he matured for his first year as a favourite of patients because of his good nature and empathic intelligence. He was a favourite of the Sisters because he was good for the patients, proved himself a capable ratter, and was just Jim, their own little bundle of brown and black joy. A bundle that was growing into a muscled, strong dog, but still a bundle to them.

But something was stirring within him, some sense of adventure, and Jim was about to embark on a whole new life, whether the Sisters liked it or not.

Jim's Sense Of Purpose

WHEN HE was about a year old, Jim disappeared from the hospital and was gone for the night. He had been allowed to roam freely, but had shown no desire to wander past the entrance lodge at any time before. The Sisters were worried about him, and probably those patients who knew he was gone. It was evening when he disappeared, so his absence was not noticed immediately. Nonetheless, the only one who wasn't worried was Jim. Even the police constable who returned him during the following morning was worried about what had happened.

Brandon Hill was the local police station and had been for a long time. It was an old building, not the most comfortable, but the centre of a beat that had a number of men who were locals and had policed the area for years. One of the walks out of the station would take whichever Constable was on that beat past the hospital.

They had been doing this long before Jim arrived and for the whole year that he had been in residence. He didn't seem to have noticed before, but on this day, for reasons known only to him and which he obviously couldn't share, Jim had decided to follow the Constable who had walked past the entrance lodge. Something had caught his eye, possibly the uniform or maybe even some scent that the Constable carried that he had not noticed before, and Jim had trotted out of the gates, into the street, and had followed the Constable on the remainder of his walk, all the way back to Brandon Hill.

The Constable had been aware of the Airedale following him and at first thought it was maybe a stray he had picked up. He had expected it to wander away, or if it was owned to go back home after a while. When it didn't, and he was back at the Station, he noticed Jim had a collar with his name and address. It was late by this time, and not wanting to disturb the Sisters unduly, he had kept Jim with him overnight at Brandon Hill, intending to return him the next morning.

Was it the keeping of Jim overnight that ignited the Airedale's curiosity? Was there something about that slightly austere and spartan building that he liked? Or did he just prefer the men at the Station to the nuns? It's impossible to know: but something just clicked for Jim. He was going to be a police dog. Whether the police liked it or not.

What Do You Mean, There Are No Police Dogs?

HAVING BEEN returned by a slightly shame-faced Constable, Jim went about his daily routine at the hospital like nothing had changed. The Sisters no doubt thought he had just got himself lost and followed the first person he could latch onto and that it wouldn't happen again. How wrong they were.

As dusk fell and a Constable passed the entrance lodge on his beat – a different Constable to the previous evening – Jim trotted out the gates and once more fell into step behind the policeman.

The following morning, the Constable returned him home. Only for Jim to repeat this again that evening. And then he started to vary his times, as if keeping an eye for any passing Constable. Up until now, he had chosen the evenings and so had walked the same beat. It was as though he had noticed that there were other Constables passing at other times of the day, and he started to keep an eye open for them. As these Constables passed the Hospital on the way to different beats, Jim started to gain a good working knowledge of the area around the Hospital and Brandon Hill station.

The Sisters, not wanting to lose their dog to the local Constabulary, and not wanting Jim to get himself lost, did their best to try and keep him in. They even started to close the gates, which was not their usual practice. All to no regard: whatever they did, Jim was more than equal to them, and he always managed to make a good escape so that he could join a Constable. He was determined to become a dog on patrol.

It was beyond explanation, and certainly not down to any

encouragement from the police, who could not understand why this bright-eyed Airedale had decided to adopt them. If anything, the presence of a dog on station premises was officially frowned upon, and so it would be a good thing for them if the Sisters could stop Jim from escaping. But despite any efforts, this continued for months, and the months became a year, and then nearly two.

Jim would not take no for an answer. He had decided to join up and become a police dog, even though there were no such animals on the Bristol Police Force. That wasn't going to stop him. For whatever instinct or intelligence had guided him, he had made up his mind that the hospital had been fine up to a point, but he preferred the company of the Constables at Brandon Hill station. And although they were good to him, and in fact had grown extremely fond of him (not that they could openly admit this), even they could not understand why he would swap his comfortable hospital for the station.

Brandon Hill had never been an attractive or comfortable building. A dour, square building of red brick, it had originally been built in 1836, when it was known as Clifton Police Station and Lock-Up House, the latter due to the three cramped cells that were in the basement.

As the area had been developed around it, the newer houses were of a more pleasing design, and so Brandon Hill stood out all the more, at an angle and on a corner, a sore thumb of a building. It's still there today, having spent the 1960s as a residential block for policemen and then as the headquarters of the Avon Wildlife Trust from 1986-2022. Exactly a century after Father O'Connell found the young Jim and, if nothing else, it should have a blue plaque and a preservation order to celebrate his importance in police dog lore.

Even if he was never, officially speaking, a trained police dog.

PD Jim, Unofficially Speaking

THE LOCAL police and the Sisters bowed to the inevitable and the iron will of Jim and by early 1925 Jim had moved himself into the station, having turned his back on the hospital. The Sisters were still his owners and licence holders, but they knew where Jim wanted to be, and they had no concerns for his safety. Nor for his health, as it was obvious that the collective of Constables at Brandon Hill had taken to Jim just as he had taken to them. They got him his own basket, and he slept in the parade room, by the Sergeant's desk. They paid for his upkeep, contributing a shilling a week each for this.

All contributions were voluntary, and all men paid, another indication of how they felt towards Jim, as their wages would vary from £3 5s to £5 10s a week depending on rank and service, with a shift averaging 10s. The national average at this time was £5, so some of the Constables would have been on less than the national average, some with families. A shilling, then, was a lot to hand out for a dog that they shouldn't even have kept there. Keeper of the Jim fund would have been PC Sims, as this Constable volunteered to feed Jim, and to give him a weekly shampoo and bath.

It was only a matter of time before Jim became fully adopted as a police dog, even if completely unofficial. To mark this, the men at the station chipped in a few more hard-earned shillings and had a collar made for Jim to replace the one with his old address. The new one had a name plate on which was inscribed: 'Jim. Police Dog Brandon Hill Station Clifton.'

There was no mistaking where he belonged now and he was determined to make the most of it.

Jim soon fell into a routine, much as the routine the rest of the policemen lived by. He preferred to go out on the beat at night and so would spend most of the day sleeping in his basket. When the night shift lined up in the parade room for their evening's orders, Jim would walk up and down in front of them, looking them up and down as if he were inspecting them, and making up his mind which Constable he would patrol with that night.

Having decided this, he would then leave and walk the beat with his chosen copper, never leaving his side until that man returned to the station at the end of the night's shift. If there was any bother, Jim would not get involved as police dogs would later do, as he had no training and no commands that he would recognise. But he was an Airedale, fiercely loyal and a tough dog. There is little doubt that he would lend his weight if his man was ever attacked. There is no record of any such events, but then how could it be recorded when he was not even supposed to be there?

His moment of glory was yet to come.

In the meantime, Jim showed himself to have some quirks. For instance, he would never choose the same Constable two days running. He worked out that their beats did not change daily and so would switch from man to man in order to cover the station's territory from boundary to boundary. He also worked out that all of these men were his friends and were responsible for him, and so he liked to show no favour. Perhaps, in fact, he just wanted to share his time with all of them. Whatever the reason, this even-handedness stood him in good stead in his moment of glory.

He went on patrol with his friends, and he was very particular about who they might be, as his other quirk showed. He was able to tell ranks apart and showed no great love for anyone other than the humble PC. By now, even though he was only an unofficial police dog, his presence was not frowned upon as the men at Brandon Hill may have feared. In truth, he was seen as a fascinating novelty, and those other ranks who were also dog men were keen to meet this unusual Airedale.

Jim's discrimination began with the other ranks stationed at Brandon Hill. He lived with the Constables, patrolled with them, and was fed and bathed by them. He was one of them. Although he slept by the Sergeant's desk in the parade room, he would not let the Sergeant make a fuss of him, and he would not respond to him.

The Inspector at the station had also tried to entice Jim into his office, and had tried to teach him commands, but to no avail. Yet the dog would respond to any of the Constables. As other men from far flung stations went out of their way to visit Brandon Hill so they could meet this unusual animal, it became apparent that if they were PCs, then Jim was only too happy to meet them; if they were Sergeants, Inspectors or above, then Jim was having none of it.

How could he tell? There are those who say that it is impossible to surmise that he recognised the distinctions in the uniforms, but why not? After all, what was it that had enticed him to follow his very first Constable?

It was not just the police who were now wondering amongst themselves how he could do this, the *Bristol Observer* ran an editorial in which it queried how he was able to tell the difference. This aspect of Jim's story became even bigger news when the *Western Daily Press* picked it up and ran a headline in May 1926 that read: 'Meet PC Jim, the Clifton Police Dog. A Dog Of Unusual Intelligence Who Can Tell A Sergeant From A Police Constable.'

What the hierarchy of the Bristol Police Force thought of this is not recorded. They had no dog section, no plans for one and, like most forces around the country at this time, had not fallen for the blandishments of Lieutenant Colonel Richardson (though there's little doubt he would have approved of Jim being an Airedale). Now they had not just the local press, but the regional press calling Jim a 'Police Dog' as if he was trained and owned by the force, and not a runaway from a group of nuns and a dog who just liked to walk the beat.

Jim was a local celebrity. His wiry black and brown frame was a well-known sight around the streets when he came out at night, and the fact that he was not an officially sanctioned police dog seemed to pass everyone by; just by force of his personality, Jim had earned himself a place in the history of Avon and Somerset – when it was formed – as the first police dog on their books, even if only by his own paw.

None of this new attention seemed to affect Jim. He continued as he always had: sleep by day, choose a copper, patrol by night, return home. Bath once a week, daily feed, ignore the Sergeant and the Inspector. The streets of the Brandon Hill beat were his, and it was becoming a well-worn routine. He had moved into the station in 1925, and it was now moving towards the Autumn of 1928. Jim was six years old, in his prime. He had been a police dog for half his life. His place in history was already assured, even though he was unaware of it.

Jim's Quick Thinking Saves A Life

THE NIGHTS were drawing in and there was a considerable chill in the air when you hit the streets on the night beat. This didn't bother Jim, as his thick and wiry Airedale coat made him perfect for night work.

The same could not be said for the Constables whose beats he shared. Thick serge uniforms provided some protection, and there was always a thick topcoat if the Sergeant was in a good mood, but the midnight chill could still cut through to the bone, even before the bleak of midwinter.

It was October, and Jim had decided that night that he would walk the beat with PC Ogborn, number 133. They set out from the station as was usual, with the Constables in a line following their Sergeant and peeling off along the route he walked as they came to the start of their own beat. This line of policemen heading out for their shift and separating gradually along the march is not seen now, but was once a regular sight when the copper went out on the beat, in the days when the roads were empty. This tradition vanished and now in London you can see some policemen using buses to get from their station to where their beat begins.

But these were different days, and when Ogborn peeled off from the line, Jim followed at his heel. They were soon well out of sight of the rest of the night shift. The early hours of the beat would be taken up by those who were on their way home after pub closing time, or those few workers who plied their trade by night. In a modern world where it seems that the city never sleeps, it's hard to imagine how quiet the residential streets of Clifton must have been.

In an age when there were no shopping centres and malls as we know them, all areas had a parade of local shops which would be closed for the night. These parades would have to be checked: lamp through the window to look inside; push the door to check that it was not unlocked, either because the shopkeeper had forgotten or – more likely – a break-in had been attempted. Ogborn would have done all of this with Jim at his back, the dog keeping an eye, an ear, and a nose alert for anything unusual.

The Airedale was a terrier whose DNA made him alert to any changes around him, and in turn he would alert the Constable he was with. Jim may not have been a trained police dog, but his very nature meant that he would slip into the position with ease.

House-breakers and shop-breakers would be the only real villains that a copper on the night beat would have to look out for. In an area like Clifton, at that time, any other crimes were few and far between, particularly at night. By the time the night shift moved into the early hours of the morning, the cold and the quiet must have made the night seem darker than usual, time dragging until you could return to the warmth of the station, dour as it was. At least whichever Constable that Jim had picked for the night's walk had the dog to talk to.

There were no witnesses as to what happened next, so we can only speculate on the exact details. There were some facts that came to light later, which fix the time at which events started, but for the most part the only people who knew exactly what occurred were PC Ogborn and Jim. Ogborn had a hazy recollection, and Jim could not tell...

The Case Of The Collapsed Constable

IT WAS half-past one in the morning when PC Ogborn had an accident that left him unconscious. Was it a case of frost forming on paving and a distracted copper slipping and failing to keep his balance? Or did he have an episode that saw him grow dizzy and lose his balance? He had no health issues that were known, and this never happened to him again. Was there an assailant that came out of the darkness? A house-breaker on his way to or from a job who blundered into the copper on the beat?

It's not known and although it's tempting to create a scenario around the event, it really has no bearing on the amazing behaviour of Jim in the aftermath. Ogborn either fell or became dizzy when he was along Wells Road. He must have gone face first, as he shattered his jaw when he hit the pavement, and was out cold.

When trying to rouse him as any dog would, by nuzzling and pushing at him, and getting no result, Jim started to bark in order to raise the alarm. We know that he was heard, as it was later reports of his barks that fix the time when the incident occurred. Yet no-one responded to the dog's cry for help. To be fair, barking dogs in the night are not uncommon, and rarely a cause for concern.

When no-one came to answer his call, Jim was decisive: leaving Ogborn, knowing in some unfathomable dog sense that he could do no more to help him and that just staying with him could be harmful to his Constable, Jim ran for Brandon Hill. He knew every street in the area as he had walked every beat for three years, he was able to take back doubles and short cuts with a sense of direction that marked out the best dogs.

The station door was closed when Jim reached his destination. He must have known that it was too heavy for him to push open. Some dogs can turn handles when trained, but either Jim had not worked this out or – as is more likely given his intelligence – he simply knew he could not perform this mechanical action. So, he did what any dog would do, and what he had done when Ogborn fell: he barked. Manically, continuously, loudly. It hadn't worked before, but this was different. Jim was a smart dog and knew that there was always someone on duty inside the station.

Inside on that night was PC Nash, number 75. Hearing the dog, and knowing Jim well enough to recognise his bark, Nash left the station desk and went outside, where he saw Jim, who was alone. He had gone out with Ogborn, and Jim never came back until morning and at the heel of that night's chosen copper.

'What are you doing here? On your own?' Nash knew immediately that something was wrong, and that it was not good if Jim had left his copper behind.

He left the station and set off down the hill to find out why Jim had turned up alone. Jim had come to the station to summon help, and he had been successful. There was only one problem: in his haste, Nash had headed off in the wrong direction. Why he did this he never said. It could have been something as simple as more haste, less speed as he didn't stop to think, or it could have been that he was running through who had been given which beat in his head, and been mistaken.

Jim had perhaps already started to lead the way and turned to see Nash headed in the opposite direction. It must have been frustrating to see that he had been so misunderstood. Anyone with a dog knows that they can get irate and annoyed when an owner can't work out what it wants.

Determined not to have come this far and not get the help he wanted for Ogborn, Jim hared after Nash and grabbed at the leg of the Constable's trousers with his teeth. As Nash tried to keep on running, he found that Jim was digging his paws in and trying to stop him.

'What the bloody hell are you doing?' Bewildered and wondering why the hell Jim was acting this way, Nash pulled his trouser leg free and tried to continue, only to find Jim jumping back and grabbing hold again. Nash pulled himself free again. It was a freezing cold night, he had run out of the station thinking that Jim was alerting him to some danger, and now the dog was trying to stop him.

'What's the matter with you?' Nash shouted. 'What about PC Ogborn? He could be in serious trouble.' Nash pulled himself free yet again, and was frustrated when Jim jumped back and got hold of his trouser leg for a third time. 'For God's sake…'

It was only later, when he had time to think, that it occurred to him that Jim had been careful not to nip Nash's leg, but only to grab his trouser leg. Airedales have strong jaws, needle sharp teeth, that's why they are good vermin hunters, and also why Jim could have inflicted a nasty wound if he hadn't been so careful.

He realised that Jim had not only been trying to halt him, as he had dug his paws in, he had also started to pull backwards. It struck Nash that Jim was trying to pull him in the opposite direction: up the hill.

'Alright, you win. What is it?' Nash stopped resisting Jim and let him lead.

Realising that he had made his point, Jim let go and turned to run back up the hill, leading the way. They had already gone some way as Jim tugged at Nash's trouser leg – although referred to as the little feller earlier in the story, it should be remembered that Jim was now about six years old, a fully grown Airedale. His back would have come up to Nash's knee, and he had a strong musculature, enough to resist a man pulling against him and win that tug of war.

He was also fast. Nash lagged behind as Jim led him to where Ogborn lay, and the dog alternately stopped or slowed as he looked back, allowing Nash to keep up with him. As they reached a corner, Jim barked before turning, and Nash knew that the dog was letting him know they had arrived.

Ogborn still lay unconscious. While Jim stood back, Nash checked Ogborn over. He knew that he had to get an ambulance, but that would mean leaving him. He had to find a telephone. There were no police callboxes that he could run to, as they were not set up in Bristol until 1932. Nash had to hope he could find someone along the Wells Road with a telephone who would respond to his frantic door to door knocking. He set off to do this, telling Jim to stay and keep guard on the unconscious Constable. Jim did this, as if knowing that he had played his part: now he could rely on Nash.

Nash got a grumpy householder with a phone to let him in – 'There'll be trouble if anything happens to PC Ogborn' - and called an ambulance. When it arrived, Ogborn was taken to hospital while Jim returned to the station with Nash.

Ogborn made a full recovery in hospital. His injuries were not life threatening, but his situation had been. In the cold, unconscious on the freezing stone of the pavement, Ogborn would have suffered from exposure. Given that it was half past one when he fell, and was unlikely to have been found by any early risers until about half past six, those five hours would have been enough for the exposure to kill him. Without Jim, he would have lain there undetected, his absence only noted when he did not return to the station at the end of his shift.

Given this, and the time it had taken Nash to find a phone and get an ambulance, every minute that Jim had spent chasing back to the station, alerting help, and getting it to the prone Constable, had been vital. If he had just sat over Ogborn, the policeman would have perished.

Jim The Hero

JIM'S INTELLIGENCE and courage in recognising the problem, finding help, and then making sure that help went in the right direction, did not go unnoticed. He was treated by the Brandon Hill boys as a hero. He was more than a dog, more than a police dog to them by now: he was one of their own.

The local press, already fond of Jim and his unique place in the life of Bristol, covered the story and declared that Ogborn's situation would have cost him his life if not for Jim. A photograph appeared in the papers of Jim striding through the streets of Bristol between two Constables, looking every inch a dog ready to spring into action. It was obviously posed: it was taken in a street during daylight, and Jim was a night-time dog; and he would hit the beat with only one Constable as there were never two on a walk. But it looked good, and is one of the few images we have of him.

In the months that followed Jim's exploits, the Mother Superior of St Mary's Hospital decided that it was about time Jim's ownership was made official. The Sisters still had affection for their little Jim, but he was not so little now and had been away from them for over half his life. It was time for them to let go, and so his official ownership was transferred as a gift from the Sisters to the Bristol Constabulary. From February 8th 1929, they now paid for his license and were officially responsible for him.

Others were keen to show their appreciation of Jim's act of courage. The Bristol Dogs Home commissioned a special silver collar and a medal which detailed Jim's loyalty. Loyalty to his comrades: that was undoubtedly how he saw them, and they him. It was a splendid gesture, but Jim still wore the collar that had been made for him by the Brandon Hill boys, proclaiming him 'Jim (Police Dog)'.

A year after that, on May 26th 1930, a specially arranged ceremony was held in honour of Jim within the Lord Mayor's Parlour at the Council House. He was presented with an engraved silver medal and a collar described as 'very beautiful' in the press. That would be two ceremonial collars, then, that would never take the place of his simple 'Police

Dog' collar, something he had always been and which he would always be.

There is a photograph of Jim laying on a table, looking intelligently beyond the camera, while the Lord Mayor and Lady Mayoress make a fuss of him, with PC's Ogborn and Nash standing behind Jim. This is the only photograph that shows Jim, the man he saved, and the man whose understanding of Jim helped this happen.

What happened to Jim? There are no further records and even Alan Vowels, the official historian, does not know. I would like to think that as he got older, one of the Constables – perhaps even Ogborn or Nash – took him in. He could not be retired as such, as he was never an official police dog, but there would come a time when his aching old bones could not walk the cold night shift anymore. It would be nice to think that Jim ended his days at the hearth of a favourite copper. If not, perhaps back at St Mary's, where the Sisters could finally reclaim him for their own.

No, Jim was never an official police dog, but he was more than that: his desire to be with the police, whatever fuelled it, showed a sense of service and a courage in action that is a benchmark for all police dogs, and one which they all live up to.

Jim's Legacy

IN ALL, you could argue that if Jim had a legacy, it went no further than his story being remembered by a few locals and some historians. Certainly, his fame did not spur the Bristol Constabulary to start a dog section or to investigate further into whether it would be advantageous to look at a dog training programme. Which, considering they were happy to take on his license when awarded it by the Sisters, shows a distinct lack of forward thinking.

But they were not alone in their hesitance to appreciate the step forward in policing that could be offered by the use of dogs.

Even the larger forces were slow to develop, so for a smaller force with a smaller budget, perhaps it is not so surprising that the future Avon and Somerset Force did not take any dogs until after World War Two. Perhaps a crucial factor in this reluctance is British Transport Police: they would have already had dogs in service at the docks and the port at Bristol. This may be why the Bristol force did not consider dogs a necessity at the time.

Which makes Jim all the more remarkable. It was a complete anomaly at a time when even those forces which had been experimenting with the use of dogs had seemed to lose interest. Jim's glory days were the late 1920s and his Mayoral commendation was 1930, still four years away from the Home Office Report that sparked the revival of interest in dogs for the police.

Jim was an amazing dog. Not just for his personality that stamped itself on the Brandon Hill boys and the whole of the city, but also because as an adult terrier he showed the kind of courage, persistence and tenacity that had been shown by his forebears in Hull in 1908. There is a thread that runs through the history of the police dog, and it's not the German Shepherd (or Alsatian) or Spaniel – the two breeds that spring to mind readily – that define this thread.

It's the tenacity of the terrier.

As for the Avon and Somerset Force, there came eventual progress, albeit slow. As we know it today, it was formed in 1974 from the merger of the former Somerset And Bath Constabulary with the Bristol Police Force and the Staple Hill Division of Gloucestershire Constabulary.

The first official police dogs in the area did not arrive until 1957 when the Bristol Police Force gained a couple of Alsatian puppies called Kyloe and Kudos.

The section came into being as much due to embarrassment as anything else, as after a young brother and sister went missing, and were then later found murdered, the Bristol Force had to borrow a dog from the Dorset Police to help track and find the missing youths.

Kyloe and Kudos were assigned to Derek Johnston and Tom Hornsby, who had been working in other sections of the Bristol Police. The dogs were bought at the sum of nine guineas each from the Surrey Force, who at this time were initiating their own breeding programme at Mount Browne.

From these two handlers, the section grew to a point where it now numbers more than 40 handlers, with general purpose dogs that are mostly German Shepherds (they have some Rottweilers too, which is not very common), and specialist Spaniels and Labradors whose training is in drugs, weapons, explosives, and cash.

Since 2016, the Avon and Somerset Force, as well as the Gloucestershire and Wiltshire Police have used The Brightside Ground and Bristol Pavillion, which is owned and used by Gloucestershire County Cricket Club, as their training facility. Their aim in doing this is to use a venue that will familiarise the dogs with real life situations and circumstances and that is very much the kind of place they will encounter in their everyday working life. Five dogs at a time are on site for the training days.

This is a long way from the days of Jim, but it's tempting to think that he would have flourished in such circumstances, given his strength of character and determination.

Devon And Cornwall: Another World

DOWN AT the foot of the UK, with few roads into the counties, harsh and difficult terrain – beautiful though it is – and a mainline railway that runs along the coast and is always at risk of flood or landfall, Devon and Cornwall have always been cut off and separate from the rest of the UK, which reflects in both the people and their attitude towards anyone outside their territory.

From earliest days, the police have used dogs down here. The forces were small and had not amalgamated when Edward Barrett of the Launceston Borough Police would take his dog out with him on patrol, using it very much as a weapon. Recalling the Constable and his dog, one elderly resident remembered that the people were 'more afraid of the dog than of the Constable'. Its breed was not recorded, but as this was in the 1860s and 70s, that's hardly surprising.

Around the same time as this, Superintendent Edward Marshall, commander of the Truro Division of the Cornwall Constabulary took his dog on beat with him. In March 1883 he was killed when his cart overturned on a steep bank and crushed him. The dog guarded his body so fiercely that no-one could get near the cart, although the dog did appear to recognise a uniform, and was less hostile to the approaching policemen.

An oddly parallel situation to that of Jim the Airedale occurred in Plymouth in 1897, when the Plymouth Borough Police were gifted a St Bernard called Colonel, donated by an exasperated owner named Alfred Maitland, who hardly saw Colonel as he had a habit of walking off and following any passing Constable (which sounds familiar). The Chief Constable, Sowerby, was gracious in accepting the dog, and his letter to Mr Maitland is quite charming, reading in part:

'*Dear Sir, I am extremely obliged to you for your kind offer to increase the strength of the police force by one more member. Your powerful dog 'Colonel' is practically a Policeman's dog already – I may say almost a Special Constable. On behalf of the Force, I accept your offer, at the same time assuring you that 'Colonel' will not suffer from any want of attention from his comrades.*'

It may not be a dog section programme, but it shows a willingness to look at the canine a few years before Lieutenant Colonel Richardson began his mission, and when dogs did not enter the thinking of most Chief Constables. Certainly, the Constabularies of the area had a more relaxed attitude towards dogs than other regions.

Jack was a dog whose breed may not have been recorded, but his informal adoption by a Constable in Devonport Dockyard from 1902 to 1911, assisting in policing the docks, ensured that he has a stone memorial with 'Always on duty' inscribed on it still to be seen on the dockyard. He was even placed on the 'Police Reserve' list to ensure his upkeep when he went blind in his last year.

In 1914, the Chief Constable of Exeter, Arthur Nicholson, gave his pet dog to a PC Bullen to aid in patrol work. The dog's name is not recorded, but his breed was: Airedale, those most reliable of dogs.

In the 1930s bloodhounds were informally used by the 'escape plan' squad, which consisted of 99 policemen, vehicles and roadblocks set up across Dartmoor by the Devon Constabulary to gather up those men hardy enough to make a break from HMP Dartmoor. In 1933 the Devon Constabulary Standing Joint Committee met to discuss the formal foundation of a dog unit. Plans which went on hold for another 22 years, the first Devon Constabulary Dog Section being headed up by a Sergeant Gator, whose first acquisitions were a Doberman called Feral and a German Shepherd called Astor, bought from Surrey Constabulary. The latter was responsible for the first arrest, in 1957 at Torquay, when he tracked a man and a woman who had robbed a taxi driver to a goods shed at Torre Railway Station.

In around 70 years we have come from the ad hoc and mostly disorganised way in which dogs were used by the police to the first glimmerings of the kind of streamlined and planned dog section programme that has given us the modern police dog. The influence of this most forward thinking sections produced the amazing animal of the post-war generation of policing.

It seems that we have already come a long way from Jim, the dog who decided that he would join the police, rather than the other way around. Because of this, and because he was an Airedale and not an Alsatian, it's doubtful he would have found a place easily in the post World War Two era. Despite that, he and his forebears for the British Transport Police in Jim, Mick, Vic and Ben, showed that a dog is fit for service no matter his breed, as long as he has the right stuff.

We end this part with the coming of the Alsatian but should never forget that the great police dogs of the early years were Airedale terriers. They have courage, tenacity, and a high intelligence. All of these things Jim showed when he saved PC Ogborn from death by exposure and gained the plaudits he deserved.

Police Constable Arthur Holman, aged 43, with famous police dog Rex III, who has over 100 arrests to his name, in June 1954

PART TWO 🐾🐾
Dogs In The Post World War Two Era

Rex III: the Archetype of a Police Dog

REX III was a superstar: feted in the press, immortalised in book, magazine and cinema. He was a dog doing his job, and doing it in a way that had not been seen before. Coming out of the Met Force, Rex was the result not just of their own development and learning, sometimes from other forces, but also of the meeting between the right dog and the right handler.

Sometimes something incredible happens: this was Rex III and his handler, PC Arthur Holman. But before this could happen, the circumstances had to be right, and a dog section had to be an organised and well-thought-out part of any police force. How did that come to be?

The Metropolitan Police

THE MET were surprisingly slow out of the blocks when it came to dogs. There may be many reasons for this. In-built to the DNA of this force was the aversion that the Peelers under Sir Robert Peel, and the Bow Street Runners before them, had to the use of dogs as blunt force instruments by the watchmen who came before. Similarly, the publicity stunt that was Topper and the farce that surrounded Charles Warren's misfire with bloodhounds did not endear any subsequent Met Commissioner to the idea of using dogs.

And yet, before the Home Office report of 1934, there had

been some mutterings at Scotland Yard about using dogs and, in 1931, there was a scheme to introduce dogs for tracking. This seemed to fade away for a few years, and so it was not until 1938 that the two black Labradors were introduced into the service, their tenure cut short by the onset of World War Two. However, something in that short space of time must have impressed the powers that be up at the yard, for as soon as the war was over, the first training facility at Imber Court was set up, modelled very much on the BTP centre at Hedon Hall.

Imber Court was initially the training centre for the Met's mounted police, and came under the charge of Sir Percy Robert Laurie, who was an army man recruited to the Met and then returned to the army during the war. He was the man responsible for the initiation of the dog training programme which was halted by hostilities, though he was long gone by the time the programme resumed.

The emphasis was very much on black Labradors to start with, as can be seen from an early photograph of a post-war Met handler, PC Albert Blake, whose dog Ping was a black Labrador identical to the two in service pre-war.

Initially, there were six Labradors, trained for assistance in handbag snatching incidents and the suppression of house-breaking. There was a lot of press surrounding them when they were put on show at the Imber Court Police Training Centre.

It's worth noting that the Met held back on the press until they had road-tested these dogs, as the press were shown the methods which had been used in the first 14 arrests, along with demonstrations of new drills which were being taught the dogs. It was a good indication of the success which the dog patrols had achieved since their first deployment that after the previous week's dog arrest in Hyde Park there had been no handbag snatching incidents reported from that area over the weekend period for the first time in years.

Following this, a further six were sent to divisions in West London after undergoing specific training to pick up human scent and lead the police to them. Reporting with these dogs were a Sergeant and five Constables who had trained with the dogs during the previous two months at Imber Court. A further part of their duty was to go out on beats in suburban London with the Constables. The press were told that the Labradors would have no aggressive duties to perform, being there purely to pick up scent and track. These Labradors were yellow, the first move away from the purely black Labrador that had been first favoured.

The Met had got off to a quick start in developing the use of dogs post-war, but their insistence on the Labrador cost them dearly as an innovative force. They turned their back on the man whose transfer to Surrey, and insistence on the use of Alsatians, changed the face of police dog training in the UK. It was a bad move, but one which they learned from quickly.

It wasn't until 1950 that the Met started to use Alsatians, as can be seen from a photograph that shows Rajah, an 18-month-old Alsatian in training with his handler, PC Roberts, taken at this time. The strength of the dog section was about to be increased from 23 dogs to a total of 35. The increase had been agreed as London was in the middle of a crimewave fuelled by what were known as 'cosh boys'. This post-war phenomenon was the result of a rise in both juvenile delinquency and still-young men who had returned from the war and did not want to return to a workaday world. They used leather coshes filled with sand or shot, and the upturn in violence in crime had led to an outcry and demands that the police be more proactive.

The result, as had happened four decades before in Glasgow,

was an overturn in the reluctance of a force to commit to the use of dogs. With no Lieutenant Colonel Richardson to hand by this time, the issue was where to find them. The desire to have a dog capable of inspiring fear in an opponent and aiding protection of the handler meant that despite the success of the Labradors in both their West London beats and in Hyde Park, the idea that there would be 'no aggressive duties' for the dog was becoming nonsense. Hence the recruitment of the Alsatian.

The Met was catching up, and with their larger budgets and higher profile than many county forces, they were able to develop the dog training facilities at Imber Court with some speed.

It was at this point that the call for officers wanting to train as handlers went out. One of those to answer was a Constable named Arthur Holman.

Surrey: Always Looking Forward

WHEN WE last left the Surrey Constabulary, they had been experimenting with the use of bloodhounds under the auspices of Inspector Tom Roberts; an experiment which had been relatively successful and would have been continued if not for the outbreak of war.

In 1946, Tom Roberts was now a Superintendent and had never stopped thinking about dogs: he was not just an excellent on the ground copper, as his promotion attested, he also had a keen analytical mind. He had continued his studies on the use of dogs in Europe before war broke out, and could see that when dogs were used there was less chance of an offender keeping close to the scene of a crime, hoping to wait out the police presence before making his escape. This statistic came readily to mind in the immediate post-war era when he was involved in a break-in where the perpetrator hid in a ditch close to the scene of the crime, waiting for the police to finish their investigation of the crime scene before making his exit. When he was eventually picked up, he made things worse by describing the police at the scene. He revealed that his method was to hide up close to his crime overnight and then slip into the morning commuter crowds as he made his way back to his London base.

Roberts reasoned that there was a double opportunity to catch the crook that had been missed. If there had been dogs on the scene to track, he would have been found. If he had elected to make his escape without waiting for morning, there would have been a good chance of his being picked up by patrols, as his crime had been in a semi-rural area. No chance there of mixing with commuters in the early hours of the morning...

If Tom Roberts was keen to push for the use of dogs once more, fate was on his side, as the new Chief Constable of Surrey appointed in 1946, Mr Joseph Simpson, was a dog man. He and his wife were Kennel Club members, and Mrs Simpson bred Labradors. So strong was their combined interest in the possibility of using dogs that Mrs Simpson later trained her Labradors for tracking and criminal work, winning trials in the civilian world.

Simpson was a strong ally for Roberts, and applied to the Home Office and the Police Authority for permission to set up a dog section with a training programme based on methods used in Europe. Permission was granted, with the proviso that the dogs used be those whose breeds were tried and tested in the field: using Germany as their model, the forward thinking Surrey team opted for Dobermans and Alsatians.

There was still some frustration as the aftermath of the war meant that resources had to be directed elsewhere until 1948. However, this was a blessing in disguise for the Surrey men, as it enabled them to find and recruit the crucial third wheel who would bring their plans to fruition.

Harry Darbyshire was a Detective Constable at the Met, and was in the Criminal Records Office at Scotland Yard. He had been in the force for 18 years and had no connection to the Met's pre-war experiment with Labradors. What he did have was a strong interest in the breeding and training of dogs, which had led him to attend a number of police dog trials, particularly in Germany, before the war. He also had his own dog, Anna Of Avondale, an Alsatian that had been a German war dog captured by the Parachute Regiment near Ashwerin, Germany, in 1945.

When the Met set up their own dog section post-war, Darbyshire applied to join as he was keen to move into a role where he could work with dogs. The Metropolitan Dog Section offered him a role training Labradors for protection, as this was to be their focus. Suggesting that they use Alsatians, Darbyshire was told that they had an unreliable temperament. This was not an uncommon view in the UK, despite evidence from the continent to the contrary, and the use of the breed by the British Transport Police, beginning at Hull Dock, from 1923 onwards. It was only the rapid success of Surrey's training programme that led to the adoption of the Alsatian by most other forces.

Learning of this, Surrey made their move, and Darbyshire was transferred from the Met to Surrey with a promotion to Sergeant. Arriving in February 1948 with Anna, he was housed in a large police house at Shackleford, with the surrounding country and a large garden which he could use to further his training programme.

Anna of Avondale is a key figure in the development of dog use in the UK. Having already been Army trained, she was primed for further training by Darbyshire, using techniques he had learned from his pre-war visits. And she was soon to prove her worth and justify the faith of Roberts and Simpson.

The Co-Op in Hersham would not appear, at first glance, to be the scene of a major breakthrough: but that was exactly what it was only a few weeks into Darbyshire's tenure. Divisions throughout Surrey had been informed of the new dog section and had greeted this with scepticism.

Despite this, the police on the scene called for Anna, and she showed her worth by picking up a scent immediately and tracking the perpetrator from the scene of the crime to where he was hiding under a hedge in a nearby garden. The speed and efficiency of Anna impressed itself immediately – while incidentally proving Tom Roberts' point about criminals hiding close to the scene – and gave a credibility to the dog section that was invaluable in its rapid growth.

Anna continued in service until she died in August 1950, and the following year the Home Office supported a trip by Tom Roberts and Harry Darbyshire to Germany in order to research training methods. This was prompted by the desire of Mr Simpson to set up a training school in Surrey that would provide not just training, but build up a pool of dogs who were considered the right breeds for the work they would undertake.

This was to be supported by a breeding programme that was the first of its kind – and indeed the only one for some years – that would supply a stream of police dogs. They could be bred from working animals and would be raised and trained as police dogs from pups. The random acquisition of dogs from a number of sources, as had been the practise for many forces, was not necessarily a bad thing: some fine dogs came this way, as we see throughout, but there was also the chance of issues arising that could be avoided by breeding. This was Darbyshire's aim in setting up a breeding programme: his belief was that a dog could only be good for the job if it was bred for it.

The desire to set up the training school was fuelled not just by the need to build their own section, but by the constant stream of Chief Constables who were thinking of setting up their own dog sections and were impressed by the rapid and successful growth down in Surrey. A growth that had been accelerated by the move for Surrey Police Headquarters from the centre of Guildford to Mount Browne in 1949.

This gave them a house with 37 acres attached, on which there were built offices and twenty houses for accommodation, as well as tennis courts, two 20 pitches, a cricket pitch, and a rifle range. Most importantly, there was still a large amount of space remaining. This gave Darbyshire all he required to build the kind of kennels and training facilities that he envisaged. Not an easy man to know, by all accounts, he was nonetheless dedicated and could be found during the day building the walls and paths for his new training school before knocking off at five and commencing training in the early evenings.

The drive to produce better and better dogs in training and in breeding was the reason that Mount Browne and Surrey feature so heavily in the history of other forces. Police dogs as we first think of them now stem from Darbyshire's insistence on Alsatians: without Surrey, the Met would not have started to use Alsatians, and Arthur Holman would never have been given Rex III...

Just Another Night?

LONDON AFTER World War Two was a very different place

to the London of today. It was littered with bomb sites and ruined buildings. There was an atmosphere of cold, hard austerity. It was bitterly cold in winter, foggy and icy, and not the kind of place where you want to hang around. This was certainly how PC Arthur Holman felt one November night when he was standing in a bombed-out house with his dog Rex III, keeping watch on a block of flats called Maitland Court. The lights from within were inviting in the weather.

Following a smash and grab raid at a radio and television shop in Cricklewood, the gang involved were chased by a radio car but had escaped in a Mark Seven Jaguar. This had been the latest in a series of raids by the gang, christened the Phantom Car Gang by newspapers. They had also raided a jeweller in Regent Street, and a radio shop in Fulham.

The Flying Squad had tracked them down to this location and now required Rex and Holman to keep watch. Holman was asked to contact Superintendent Peck, the officer in charge of the dog section. He was told to contact the Flying Squad. They needed a dog as the men they were after were known to be dangerous and not afraid to use violence. The Jaguar, which had been stolen from Piccadilly, was now kept in a lock-up at Maitland Court in Addison Road, Notting Hill. This was the first time the squad had asked for help from a dog. The choice of Rex was proof that he was the finest dog in the force.

Holman had been picked up from his home in Mitcham by a squad car and deposited by a roofless, bombed out house. This was their lookout post: having climbed to the top storey, Rex was motionless and silent beside his handler as it began to rain. Rex had a pat and then licked Holman's hand. He understood he had to stay there. There was no sign of them for a while. Satisfied there would be no action tonight, Rex jumped to his feet, shook himself and bounded down ahead of Holman on the stairs, tail wagging like a metronome as they were standing down.

The following evening, it was frosty and icy. Rex sat quietly. A car left the garage. They would wait until the car returned. It went out at around 8.00pm and returned at 10.30pm. When it was in the garage, Holman and Rex went down to the street. He was in plain clothes, so all anyone would see was a man taking his dog for a walk.

As he walked past the flats, two men came out. A plainclothes officer came running to apprehend the crooks. As others came from the opposite direction, one of the two men spun around and ran down a nearby side-turning. The first was taken down, but the other ran away, and Holman and Rex were on the far side of the action.

Holman gave the command. He knew that because of Rex's training he would ignore the men still struggling on the ground. The dog overtook them and chased greyhound-swift after the fleeing villain. As the man scrambled over a six-foot gate set in a wall, Rex jumped onto the top of the wall, skidding on its icy surface and paying no heed to the 18-foot drop on the other side.

Man and dog disappeared as Rex followed him over the gate, and by the time Holman had climbed the gate it was all over. The suspect had fallen over against some dustbins and Rex had the lapel of the man's coat firmly in his teeth. Holman had ordered Rex to release his grip and marched the man back to the gate, ordering him to climb back over. The man smiled at him, and as he landed on the other side with Holman at his back he tried to get away once again.

Some people never learn. Rex was too much for him as the dog grabbed him and dragged him back once again. When they reached the street, two more men came from the lock-up.

They took one look at the police and prisoners and started to flee. Holman was told to stop them and again Rex sped after the men, disappearing into the darkness of Addison Road. He stopped the first man by leaping on his back and pushing him to the ground, and as Holman apprehended him Rex went hurtling after the second crook, seizing his wrist in his teeth to detain him.

Presently, four prisoners were lined up against the wall, guarded by policeman and dog. Rex was under command to watch them closely while Holman went to a nearby house to try and find a telephone. The Flying Squad men had gone to check the lock-up. Unable to find a phone – this was less than 10 years after World War Two after all, and telephones were still not common in some areas – one of the squad men went to stop a car.

At this distraction, one of the prisoners dived across the yard at the side of the flats and darted down to cross the gardens beyond. Holman commanded 'stop him' and Rex did not let him down. He disappeared over the wall in pursuit with Holman close behind. He found Rex standing over the prone body of the prisoner, teeth bared and growling.

The Flying Squad eventually found a motorist who sought out a call box and dialled 999. Ten minutes later they were safely inside Notting Hill Gate police station. In the back of the Jaguar, they found a silver rose bowl and several silver challenge cups worth £500. The leader of the gang was what was colloquially called a right villain, but he was not unlikeable and after he was formally charged, he said to Holman, 'No copper could catch me but if you're going to teach dogs to do that then I'm going straight.' He didn't – the gang went to prison for four years, two years and 18 months respectively and not long after coming out, the gang leader was soon back inside. Rex received a commendation from the judge and Holman gave him an extra portion of his favourite dinner: fresh cooked liver.

It had been just another night's work for Rex.

The Ideal Police Dog

REX III was possibly the most renowned British police dog; certainly, he's the only police dog in the UK to have a film made about him. *Police Dog* from 1955 is a terrible British B-Movie. It's not worth watching unless you have a lot of patience waiting for when the dog appears – as Rex III plays himself – but it is worth noting as an example of how Rex entered the public consciousness and shaped how we imagine police dogs to be. Even these days, some 70 years later…

When we think of general-purpose police dogs we think primarily of Alsatians. Rex is the reason for this. His handsome appearance, courage and intelligence are what made him famous. He was the best thief-taker of his day. He made 120 arrests. He was the first dog to help with the Flying Squad and the first dog trained to detect drugs by the Metropolitan Police. He also proved dogs could be used to track bandits in the Malayan jungle during the Malayan war of the 1950s. His handler, PC Arthur Holman considered him the finest dog that he'd encountered. Rex's fame was such that a cartoon strip about his exploits which appeared in the magazine 'Look and Learn' in the 1950s was still being republished over 20 years later, when Rex was nothing more than a memory.

Rex never got the chance to retire: at seven years old he developed throat cancer and had to be put down. Holman was heartbroken, and the police lost a talisman.

Shortly after, Rex got his own memorial when Holman published *My Dog Rex*, paperbacked under the more dramatic title 'Dog Vs Crime'. It's a fitting tribute, the first time a police dog had a book devoted to his life, and something that cemented the legend of Rex III and the idea of the Alsatian as the definitive police dog.

The Early Days

POST WORLD War Two the dog sections in all the forces around the country realised that we were entering a new world. Up until this time, the dog sections were haphazard and they were often poorly organised, coming into existence almost by accident.

Post World War Two, the Metropolitan Police established their training centre at Keston. This became a benchmark, following as it did the Surrey police dog section training ground. Surrey and the Met were the two forces that subsequently put the most work into developing the breeding of dogs and the training of them in specialist kennels.

Just as the Met police had Keston, Surrey Police had Mount Browne which was a 37-acre site with kennels and training facilities. The West Midlands police force had introduced their first dog, PD Don, at Walsall in August 1939, shortly before the outbreak of World War Two. This put a hold on their plans, and it was not until 1951 that they had their first dog handler, with PD Flash in Birmingham. Coventry followed suit 10 years later, and gradually the use of dogs across the midlands became more unified.

In Hampshire, Southampton was the first police force within the Hampshire Constabulary to appoint dog handlers, PCs Jack Ryles and Ron French with their dogs Quaker and Wendy, in 1952. Forces such as Hertfordshire and Glasgow had, as we have already seen, been developing their dog sections since the early years of the century, but again, after the war, this was stepped up. Somerset and Avon did not introduce dogs for some time, although a dog did introduce himself to them, as we know.

Surrey, it should be noted, first introduced dog use during World War One, but again this was not really organised until the post-war period. In many ways it was only when the Met decided to adopt a dog section, initially in 1931, that other forces began to take the idea of such a section seriously, even if the Met's own progress was of a haphazard nature. Some gathered dogs almost at random, some bought in dogs, and some toyed with the idea of specific breeding programmes. It was not, as yet, co-ordinated in any way.

At the time, due to the haphazard nature of its development, it must have been a nightmare for any police officer looking to plan a programme of coordinated training and development. That dog sections became the force they are now can seem at times almost astounding.

The work of Surrey and its adaptation by the Met are the two most important factors in the dog section as we see it now. And if there is one dog that takes all this seemingly random activity and becomes the focus and catalyst for how the public viewed the police dog, and so how the force came to mirror that perception, then it can be seen in one canine form: Rex.

Rex was a purebred for the force, even if not actually bred by them, and his induction into that force actually followed the common pattern of being a giveaway.

After World War Two, PC Holman was attached to CID as an aid to the Ghost Squad, carrying out undercover observations in South London. In early 1950, Scotland Yard asked for volunteers who had previous experience with dogs. They were planning an experiment in the training of dogs to assist in the detection of crime, something that had begun before the war but had been put on hold. Holman didn't think twice about this, and his name was put down immediately.

Soon afterwards he was told he could collect his dog from Imber Court which is where training initially took place before Keston was opened. There were three dogs available, and three new handlers. Holman had already owned two dogs called Rex as pets, and so he had no problem making his choice. From the point of view that Rex was the oldest of the dogs, this may not have been a wise choice as it was believed that the older a dog, the harder it would be to train. Whoever chose Rex will be taking on a dangerous handful, he was warned.

However, as soon as Holman saw him, he knew he hadn't made a mistake. People who've never had an animal think a dog is just a dog. This is not the case. Holman felt a thrill of excitement that shot through him when he saw Rex was indeed a king amongst dogs: an Alsatian, large, with black and tan markings, clear brown eyes, and sharply-defined, intelligent features. Holman could feel a vital force that emanated from him. Holman noted that Rex was as hard and fit as they come, all bone and muscle, with a perfectly conditioned, shining coat.

The terms of the dog's licence for ownership were simply that Holman had to catch thieves with him, and indeed they did. In total, Rex made 125 arrests throughout his career and although his licence was technically held by the Metropolitan Police, he was Holman's dog, free to live with him, was trained and handled by him, operated only by him, would never eat unless fed by him, and not obey a single order that was not given by Holman.

Rex's induction into the police force was almost accidental, as he was born in March 1949 and as a pup was kept with the watchman at the French Legation Company. However, he fell victim to automation when the Legation installed automatic burglar alarms, and so, when he was a year old in 1950, he was given to the Metropolitan Police.

The first morning he had him, Holman groomed him with a brush and comb that he had kept from the days of his second dog named Rex. And for the rest of this Rex's life, he never went out on a night patrol without first having a run, or a day patrol without first having a grooming. Except, of course, for those occasions when they were unexpectedly called out in the middle of the night. This did seem to happen quite a lot, as Rex was the go-to dog for results. Holman accepted this as a part of the job and as a badge of honour as it showed how respected Rex had become. Holman's wife on the other hand never got used to the disturbed sleep even though she adored her 'Rexy'.

Training

DURING THE three months of intensive training that Rex and Holman undertook, a van arrived and would take them to work, depositing them back home at the end of each nine-to-five day. Although Rex was a quick study, the initial stages were surprisingly difficult as the dog did not take easily to a chain and collar, refusing to respond when they were on, and it took some time to get him used to them. Holman did wonder if Rex would ever be trainable if he couldn't get beyond that basic command. It was during this time that he noticed a wet patch develop on Rex's side.

Examining him, he could see he had a wound where a sliver of glass had got under his collar during training and worked its way down under the skin, settling between the ribs. The reluctance for the collar became clear. Even worse for Rex, he did not like being taken to the vet for this, and on those rare occasions when he saw the vet afterwards, he would always go for him. A dog never forgets.

However, once he got past this initial hurdle, Rex learned commands like 'sit' quite easily, and it wasn't long before they experimented with him chasing a criminal. A fellow policeman would play the supposed criminal. He would run away from Holman and as he ran Holman would call 'stop him' with a wave of the hand. Rex would then give chase and catch the fake criminal's arm. He would not let go until he was pulled away and told to leave. Eventually, 'leave' on its own would make him stop.

One thing Holman was concerned about with this was that the command 'stop him', to send Rex after someone, could mean that Rex may just stop whoever was in front of him, regardless of who it was. However, Rex seemed to have an uncanny gift for recognising people who were friends, in and out of uniform.

To illustrate this, early on in Rex's working life, they were in Battersea looking for a man who'd taken part in a smash and grab raid on a mackintosh shop. Holman spotted him running down a side turning and ordered 'stop him'. Rex was out of the car they were in before Holman could even open the door. By chance, another man came running out of the night, diagonally across the path of the man with the coats and Rex, put off by the appearance of this second person, jumped at him. However, a quick 'no' made him swerve away from the innocent passer-by and after the real criminal, who he caught up with swiftly.

It was important to teach him to obey only Holman's voice. Otherwise, anyone could say 'sit' and get him to leave a criminal he was chasing. Interestingly, he found Rex was easier to train off lead than on lead (which may go hand in hand with his earlier dislike of the collar and chain) and he was always a very good and very responsive dog who would never move unless he was told.

One of the fascinating things about this era is that there was no training program as such. It was down to Holman to devise a program himself. For instance, when he was teaching Rex to track, he would duck behind a tree and lie flat on the ground, not letting the dog know he had done this. Rex would go on regardless and then have to track back and find Holman after he turned and found his handler was no longer there.

Other handlers in tracking training tended to use the phrase 'seek' to send a dog off, whereas Holman preferred to use the phrase 'find him'. His reasoning was simple: this way, he could make sure that Rex would respond only to certain words that could come from him. The command was definite. It was a tactic that would ensure Rex was never confused by attempts to counter commands, even as he knew only to obey Holman's voice.

Rex was a very good jumper and hurdler, which is something that not a lot of dogs have. He was an extremely strong animal throughout his life. It was also very important that Rex should not accept food from anyone other than his handler. For one thing, he could be poisoned; for another, he could be kicked or bludgeoned while busy eating. It might sound ridiculous, but there have been many guard dogs on site that have fallen in this way. So, Holman trained him by using one of his colleagues as an assistant.

The mission was for Rex to not accept food from anyone else. This was done by getting someone to offer food and if Rex went to take it, he was not given the food but given a light flick at his nose. This may sound cruel, but a light flick with no pain was a signal that would soon be learned. And a vital one. Mind you, Holman kept him on a rope at this point to prevent him attacking the person who annoyed him.

One day, a fellow policeman started tormenting Rex with the food and flick trick and thought it was immensely funny. Holman was not present when this started, and when he returned the man had tired of this and was some distance away. Rex was released for a run, and he ran straight towards his tormentor, sinking his teeth hard into the seat of the victim's trousers.

Rex was ordered to 'leave', and at first a baffled Holman was unable to understand what had happened. Had his dog shown a side of himself that would be unsafe? This feeling persisted until he was told by other policemen what this man had been doing. He then felt Rex deserved a pat rather than punishment, as no animal likes to be humiliated, and Rex was able to retaliate with something more than an irate lap dog could show.

Training for tracking continued by taking him onto Esher common (where Imber Court was based) and using other policemen who were friends to lay a trial. Holman also used his wife on Mitcham common, where he lived, for this and interestingly Rex found it harder at first to follow her. It transpired her perfume was the issue here, and all it needed was practice.

There was nothing wrong with his nose for a scent. Early in his training when he was tracking a fellow dog handler called McCallum, a number of people crossed the trail ahead. Rex, nonetheless, kept the policeman's scent despite the confusion. Daily, the people he was sent to track were given longer and longer starts across more varied terrain, until eventually he could lead Holman to someone who had started off more than an hour and a half earlier.

Rex was also taught to retrieve and fetch. The primary problem with training here was in trying to make sure the dog did not try to eat or swallow any of the objects. This practice of fetching was common then, but as we have seen, is in contrast to the modern practice of getting the dog to find and stay with the object because of the increase in forensic capabilities.

Rex Starts Work

REX PASSED his training in July 1950. Holman went back to work, now with Rex. His station was in W division, south of the Thames. The first morning back at the station, he was astounded to find that, as he went to Rex's kennel in the garden, the dog growled at him. At first, he didn't understand this, and then he realised that he was in his police uniform: throughout all of Rex's training at Imber Court, Holman had worn civilian clothes. As soon as Rex understood the uniform, everything was fine.

They were stared at on their way to the station as police dogs were still very much a rarity. The local press even ran a story about Rex because of this. From then on, as further stories recorded the arrests he made, Holman could have walked through the streets dressed like an Emperor, and no one would have noticed: they only had eyes for the dog.

There were some early incidents where people allowed their dogs to attack Rex or try and fight with him. Part of this was down to owners who could not control their dogs, although there was a small group of people who secretly wanted to see if their dog could get the better of a police dog.

Rex was always going to come off best, and Holman was more concerned that he would have irate owners complaining than of any injury to Rex. However, as people got more and more used to seeing Rex around, they knew better than to let their dogs near him.

Night Service At The Garage

IT WAS more than a month before Rex had a chance to prove himself in action. They were patrolling Sutton in a wireless car one night when a call came through, directing them down to the Sutton bypass. They arrived just as an ambulance was pulling out from the kerb, and Holman's immediate impression was that there had been a minor explosion.

In fact, what they had before them were tyre marks half-hidden by a semi-circle of men and women clustered around an overturned motor car. After closing time at a local pub, two owners had agreed to race home. Going at speed, one of them hit an obelisk in the centre of the road and skidded onto the pavement and through 30 yards of front gardens. The occupants were alive, though badly injured. Their task from the radio car was to arrange removal of the smashed saloon.

Holman went down to the Phoenix garage in Sutton where there was an all-night breakdown service. But the man in charge was the only one on duty. 'Who's going to look after this place if I go?' he asked.

Holman told him, 'I will. With Rex, of course.'

So, they made themselves comfortable in the garage office. There were no customers, but there must have been some hitch in picking up the wrecked car as at three in the morning he still hadn't returned. It was then that Rex, quiet up to that point, jumped up. His hackles were up and he was quivering. Holman listened but couldn't hear anything. However, he knew that Rex had picked up some sound, so they both went out to the forecourt. There was a low wall and he told Rex to sit down behind the wall, in the forecourt but shielded from the road.

A few seconds later, two men came from a side street, each carrying a sack. Holman went over to them.

He said, 'I'm a police officer and I'd like to know what you're doing at this hour of the night with those sacks.'

One of them, a large man, replied that they had just come from Joe's. Holman asked him who Joe might be.

'A friend,' he replied.

Holman told them that he wanted to see what was in the sacks. They hesitated, then at a signal from the larger man, they both dropped the sacks from their shoulders. By this time, Holman had recognised the larger man as a housebreaker who had already been through police hands. Warily, he looked into the sacks where all he saw was a large number of vegetables.

'Where does this come from?' he asked.

'Joe's' was the response, but uttered in a tone of voice that suggested trouble.

Holman made a decision. Rationing was still in use and large amounts of food like this on the black market had a decent value for a night's thieving.

'You're coming down the station,' he told them.

The large man squared himself. 'I don't think you're taking us anywhere,' he said, knowing there were two of them and only one copper. That attitude changed immediately when Holman hailed Rex and the dog bounded over the wall and rushed across to them. The large man stepped down. 'Alright,' he said, 'if you want us to come, we will. But put that damned dog on a lead.'

Holman told them to pick up the sacks and follow him down to the nearest police box – the only form of contact with head-quarters for a copper on the streets before two-way radio and then mobile phone tech – and when they reached there, he told Rex to guard them while he made the call. Neither man moved until a car arrived to take them to Sutton police station. While they were there, the crew of the wireless car that had originally taken Holman and Rex to the crash scene arrived. The driver looked at them, astonished. 'Where the hell have you been, and what the hell have you got there?' he asked.

'A couple of blokes who've done over a greengrocer's,' Holman replied, leaving the driver to work out how they had got from a garage to a greengrocers.

The answer, of course, was Rex's remarkable hearing, without which they may have passed Holman by while he was in the garage office. It was only going outside and following his dog that allowed him to spot them.

Rex's Reputation Spreads

THE DEMAND soon became 'Get Holman, I want that dog from Tooting'. This was how he became responsible for the capture of South London's Ram gang. They were called this because their procedure was clumsy, but effective. They would steal a car, drive it to a large tobacconist, park up on the pavement, then break down the shop door with a small battering ram before filling the car with cigarettes and driving off. They worked fast, chose deserted roads early in the morning, and so made a number of successful raids. At 2:31 one morning an Inspector from Balham police station saw a car outside of a tobacconist shop near a housing estate. Three men were hurrying out. He found a police box and asked for Rex.

At the same time, Holman was awoken by Rex's barking: this became his early warning for the approach of a police car on call-out for him. Dressing quickly, he collected the dog, and they were soon on the way, outside the tobacconist in less than 20 minutes. Having been spotted, the thieves had left the car and scattered into the night. Holman put Rex on a tracking

REX III: THE ARCHETYPE OF A POLICE DOG

line, an extra-long lead necessary to prevent him rushing off into the blackness of the night without Holman being able to see where he had gone. It also gave him the length and necessary give to move about and turn on his tracks without straining at his collar.

Holman took Rex over to the car and ordered him to track. Rex sniffed for a couple of seconds, then led Holman back across the road, his nose to the ground, down a side turning and through some back alleys. Occasionally he stopped, doubled back to confirm his trail, picked up his scent, and then strained on. He came to a low fence and leapt over it. He skirted the back of a house and reached an outside lavatory. He began to bark. Holman opened the door and found a Teddy Boy (the juvenile delinquent of the time) cowering against the wall. 'Take that dog away,' he sobbed, 'take that dog away…'

Holman took the thief back to the car and the other officers. Then he commanded Rex to track again. Rex set off down through a maze of prefabs (temporary housing of the day) and through a passageway before attempting to jump an eight-foot chain-link fence topped with barbed wire. Holman steadied him and stopped him trying again. Instead, he tried to lift the bottom of the fence to allow Rex to get underneath, but the space he could make was too tight for the dog.

The wire fence made three sides of a square, and the fourth side was the back of some houses. He told the other policemen who had followed that someone had better knock up the people in one of the houses. 'Go through those back gardens and you've got him,' he said. The other policeman looked at him.

One of them said, 'We can't wake people up at this hour.'

Holman was astonished. He looked at Rex. 'If you can't, I will,' he said, determined Rex's work should not go to waste.

111

Admonished, the policemen clattered off, leaving Rex and Holman on guard in case the crook attempted to break out as they had got in. They nabbed him in one of the houses, and went back to the car, but unfortunately there were too many cross scents now, and Rex could not follow the third man. Two out of three was not a bad haul, however, as without him it would have been none out of three.

Children And Dogs Who Are Not Quite Lost

A HOT CLOUDLESS day in August 1951, perfect weather for the crowds at Mitcham Fair. Hurdy Gurdy sideshows and roundabouts. Rex had been given a run over the common and golf course and stopped to watch the joy of the fair, hoping there would be no incidents to mar it. Holman was on duty and placed Rex in a shady patch under a tree and told him to stay while Holman walked over towards the caravans in which the showmen had their living quarters. An old Gypsy fortune teller came from the tent and walked up to him. But she wasn't looking at him: she was looking at Rex.

'It's a shame that such a good-looking dog is allowed to stray,' she said. When Holman agreed, adding that perhaps you'd think its owner would look after it. She gave him a look and then said, 'It's a lovely animal. Do you think I could keep it? I need a dog for my caravan.'

Holman shrugged and said, 'Go over and stroke him. See if he'll go with you. If he does, I don't see why you shouldn't have him.' The Gypsy walked over to Rex and stroked him. He opened one eye and yawned. 'He doesn't seem to be savage,' she said. She looked around and added, 'They'll never find him once I get him in my caravan.'

And then, as she probed through the dog's ruff, she found

his collar and name plate, which had the words Metropolitan Police on it. 'It's a police dog,' she said, 'we've heard about him. What are we going to do with him? Should I take him to the station? Would there be a reward?'

'A good idea,' Holman said. 'You take him, if he'll go.'

She stared at Holman suspiciously and then realised that he was a policeman and not someone from the Brass Band, or the local gas board. She had been fooled by the fact that Holman was wearing a flat cap, which had been adopted by the dog section when all other policemen were wearing helmets. How wrong she was, and how annoyed she was, swearing at him as he collected Rex and went about his duties, laughing to himself.

Shortly after this, an evening patrol was interrupted by a police car, pulling up quickly beside Holman and Rex. A child was missing, they told him, and they wanted Rex to find her. Missing child cases were always worrying, not just for the reasons that we think of now, but also because London in the early 1950s was still littered with bomb sites and derelict, unsafe buildings, as well as building sites attempting to remake the capital.

When they went to the child's home, in the Clapham area, they knew that she had been seen recently near a building site. The girl's father, a distraught little man, was pacing outside the house along with a group of policemen. The local station Inspector told Holman that they had made a thorough search of the area, particularly the building site, with no sign of anyone. He added that so many people would have passed by it would be impossible for Rex to track without knowing which particular scent he should follow.

Holman asked if they had anything handled by the girl. The Inspector had already thought of this and handed Holman one of her dresses. Rex sniffed this and Holman ordered 'Track'. Rex circled for about 30 seconds, which was a long time for him, and then suddenly he was off.

He ran along the centre of the pavement, curved inward and passed some sweet and cake shops which she probably visited, then deviated through some Hopscotch squares before resuming the middle of the pavement, down through a number of side turnings before at last stopping before a garden gate...

He had come back to the house where he started.

'But this is where she lives,' the father yelled.

'Are you sure the child's not inside?' Holman asked him.

The man went red with anger and said, 'If your dog's no good admit it, but don't tell me I don't know if my kid's at home or not. What do you think I am?'

Holman let this pass but still couldn't understand why Rex had doubled back. 'I'm going to have a look around,' he told the Inspector. Starting with the housing site, Holman and Rex made a thorough search of the building site and all the area around. After two hours he reported back to the inspector, who was on his own now.

'I'm convinced the dog wasn't wrong,' Holman said, 'have you been inside and looked?'

The Inspector said he hadn't, but at Holman's urging he went inside and looked. Five minutes later, he returned grinning. 'Would you believe it?' he said. 'The kid is inside. She's been there all the time. She's fast asleep in bed.'

'But how could that happen?' Holman asked.

The Inspector grinned. 'He's got 14 kids. The answer's simple, he can't add up. Amazing, isn't it, it took a dog to count his children for him...'

REX III: THE ARCHETYPE OF A POLICE DOG

The Cold River, The Colder Trail

IT HAD been an icy cold day that December and it was now a freezing night. Holman's wife hoped that he wouldn't be called out, as once he was gone, and by the time he got back, she had trouble getting warm again. Unfortunately for her, at 4:30 in the morning, Rex began barking. Holman grabbed his clothes, his boots, and the dog's tracking line. As they got in the car, he asked the driver where they were going. He was told that a safe had been burnt open at Kingsley Street, Battersea, by the Thames. The premises of Dorman Long, the construction engineers, had been raided.

The roads were glassy with ice and it started to snow as they drove. They arrived at 4:55 to find there were some 30 or 40 policemen assembled outside, many of them plainclothes CID men. Every eye was on them as they arrived: some amused, others questioning, some hostile. One of the hostile ones muttered, 'What's the use in calling in a blasted dog?' as they passed.

Holman didn't answer this. He waited until the Inspector approached and asked what had happened? He was told that three men were disturbed by the Nightwatchman at about 2:50. With some audacity, they had burned a hole in the safe with one of the firm's own oxyacetylene burners, which they ran from the offices to the yard at the back. And although the police had been searching since 3:00, they had not found a soul. The Inspector asked if Holman thought the dog could help before adding, 'I think they've gone,' which didn't inspire confidence.

But Holman had faith in Rex. He told the Inspector to get everyone out of the yard, as he didn't want Rex inadvertently attacking a detective. Once the yard was cleared, it was

115

now Holman's dog versus the efforts of 40 policemen. He had something to prove. He took Rex to the gateway of the enormous yard, which was littered with enough packing cases, metal and debris for 100 places of concealment. The police had already spent about two hours combing through this, and in the neighbouring area: now it was Rex's turn. If the safebreakers had already made good their escape, there would be no result. But if they were around and Rex didn't discover them, then the loss of prestige would be irreversible.

On the other hand, if he did find them…

Holman looked at the assembled detectives and took a deep breath. Gave Rex a pat and said, 'Good dog, find him.'

It would have been laughable if it hadn't been so ridiculous. Rex raced no more than 30 yards before he skidded to a halt and started barking. Holman joined him, looked up, and saw a man lying along the arm of a small crane: he must have had a panoramic view of the policemen searching for him. Holman got him down and said, 'What are you doing here?'

The man shrugged, 'I was looking for driftwood on the foreshore of the river.'

Holman shook his head. 'Well, you needn't have stayed up there. The tide's been out for ages.' With which, he grasped the man's arm and marched him to the Inspector. 'This looks like one of them?' he asked to gasps of astonishment and disbelieving, if blasphemous, expressions.

The Inspector said, 'You haven't been gone a minute.'

'Thank Rex,' Holman said before they returned to search for the other two men. They didn't find anyone in the yard, but Rex picked up a scent which led him across Nine Elms Lane, over a fence and along the river. It was a deep black freezing night, and the cold was bone numbing. Every single step hurt as Holman tripped and stumbled after Rex through goods yards, dumps and bomb sites. They went upriver and negotiated more than a score of obstacles.

And then the scents stopped dead. Returning to the Dorman Long yard, something occurred to Holman. He asked if the Inspector's men had worked upriver. When he was told they had, he realised that Rex had followed their scent, having no indication of which ones he should follow.

'How about downriver?' he asked.

The Inspector told him they had searched there, adding that at least the dog had caught one of them. But Holman still remembered what he had heard: 'What's the use in calling in a blasted dog?'

Holman told the Inspector that they hadn't finished yet, they were going downriver. It was even colder now, but that didn't bother Rex. He showed no signs of fatigue as they made their way across an area that was even worse for hazards than the one before. Accompanied by another policeman, Holman helped Rex across the wall of a soap factory and followed him into a yard on the other side. 'Good dog. Find him,' he said.

Rex was away in the dark. The beam of Holman's torch was like a solid line of light in the darkness as it followed Rex's progress. The dog reached a steel ladder and tried to climb up it, but he kept slipping where the rungs had iced over. Holman asked if there was any other way that he and Rex could get to the roof of the building other than the ladder?

His colleagues were dismissive, saying there was, but they had already searched up there. Holman knew that Rex was insistent as he must have followed a scent. He decided to climb the ladder himself, feeling the intense cold burn into the skin on his hands as he climbed. The pain was indescribable, but he did not stop: he had absolute trust in Rex.

He reached the top. The factory roof was large, made of glass, and as his eyes strained into the night, he could see two figures crouched behind a low wall on the far side. He skidded down the ladder and went into the factory, leaving two men outside and taking two in with him. Rex led them up the interior staircase and on to the roof. Holman bent down: 'Good dog. Find them.'

Within seconds Rex was barking and growling at them behind the wall. One of them screamed for Holman to call the dog off as he was afraid of it. He added that he'd had enough of a shock already when the safe blew back. Some people are obviously not cut out for villainy…

Once the culprits were taken to Nine Elms police station, they were searched and charged. It became apparent that it was not by some happy chance that they knew where to find the oxyacetylene gear, as two of those charged had previously worked for Dorman Long and so had decided to take advantage of what is termed 'local knowledge'.

Nine Elms was not in W division, but came under L division, and the local Chief Superintendent came down to congratulate Rex on what he called an excellent piece of detection. By now, after formalities and charging, the morning was well advanced, and Holman had no time to change into his uniform before going to Southwestern Magistrates Court in Balham High Road. The magistrate was Mr. Clyde Wilson and after remanding the prisoners in custody, he asked, 'Bring me that very useful and intelligent dog into court.'

He looked at Rex for half a minute, nodded his approval and patted him. He asked Holman several questions about him. Afterwards, whenever Holman went into his court, Mr. Wilson would always ask, 'How is Rex these days?'

After a second appearance at South London, the men were committed for trial at the Old Bailey and Rex made history as the first ever canine witness called to appear at the Central Criminal Court. Holman and Rex went along in case the prisoners alleged that Rex had bitten or savaged them, in which event Holman would demonstrate to the jury that Rex would only turn nasty when ordered to, or in self-defence. As the defendants pleaded guilty, he was not as needed in the event.

However, the national newspapers carried pictures of Rex and Holman at the Old Bailey, and fan mail started to arrive by the sackload. There were notes of congratulation, requests for photographs, for paw mark autographs from Rex, and offers of money to mate Rex with other people's Alsatians. One little girl asked for a lock of Rex's hair, and Holman cut a tuft of the dog's fur to send to her.

The Dangers Of the Cold Steel Rail

DOG HANDLING was never without its dangers, but there were some that had nothing to do with criminals and were a result of the conditions in post-war London. A good demonstration of this occurred when Holman and Rex were called out to the Clapham Junction Goods Yard at 2pm one morning just before Christmas 1952. A signal man from his box had seen someone tampering with a goods wagon. In black market post-war London, this was a regular hazard. The signal man called the police, Rex was summoned and, once in the yard, Holman ordered Rex to 'Find him.'

After the war, most goods transport was by rail, and the yards and sidings of the larger junctions like Clapham and Stratford were not the well-lit and computerised yards that we have now. Light came mostly from the lamps of the men and the trains that rumbled around the tracks, the signal men guided by their eyes, the whistles of trains, and the paper timetables they lived by. It was a safe environment if you knew what you were doing, but a copper and his dog called out and unused to the surroundings ran an extra risk.

At Holman's command, Rex raced off and Holman followed, stumbling across the railway lines. Away from the signal box the night was black and lonely. And when he looked over his shoulder at the semicircle of twinkling lights receding into the distance, he felt like a swimmer being swept further and further from shore. Railway lines, sleepers, the stones between them, and the low wires set only a few inches above the ground on the upright posts of signals: these hazards made progress difficult, especially as Holman didn't have a torch. He soon found himself tripping and cursing over a maze of lines in the centre of one of the largest railway junctions in the world.

As he stumbled, Holman heard a train approaching from behind. He turned and could see it bearing down, sparks spitting from its wheels. He realised it was a passenger express, and from the sparks that they had not just left the sidings but were somewhere among the newly electrified tracks. Rex might be killed, he thought - I must get to him. It says much about the relationship between dog and handler that when Holman came to recall it later, his first thought was for Rex. He was more than just a dog; he was a part of Holman. The same can be said to be true for almost all handlers, then and now.

I have to get him, Holman thought: suppose he treads on an electric rail? I can't leave him out there... He was trembling with fear as the dog bounded to his side. He grabbed him by the scruff of the neck and pulled him close. He took a couple of seconds to get his bearings. The train was still some way off, but where should he go now? Should he move or stay where he was? He was now between two tracks, but how close would the train be?

REX III: THE ARCHETYPE OF A POLICE DOG

A beam of light swung across the darkness and spotlighted them. 'Keep still,' screamed a voice, 'for God's sake, keep still.' In truth, Holman felt he was too paralysed with fear to move, even if he wanted to. Clasping Rex tightly, he closed his eyes. The train thundered past on the line to his left with a blast of air that nearly knocked them over. 'Keep still,' the voice roared again, 'we're coming to you.' The old foreman reached them from the dark, his concerned face bobbing up and down with the light from a lantern. 'You were lucky. You were both damn lucky. It was a miracle,' he said. 'How close you were to treading on the live rail…'

By the time they had reached a signal box, Holman had lost much of his enthusiasm for thief chasing and felt the need of a large stiff drink instead.

Rex As Display Dog

REX'S REPUTATION was such that he was put in demonstrations of police dog tactics and procedure. In 1952, Holman and Rex were sent to the Senior Police College at Dunsmore, near Coventry to perform in front of King George VI and Queen Elizabeth. These demonstrations always followed a particular pattern, in that they were designed to demonstrate all the things a police dog would do in the line of duty – track, retrieve, apprehend – to be completed in this instance by a gun chase, seeking an armed man who was hiding in a tree near to where the Royal Party were seated. This, Rex would undertake alone.

Queen Elizabeth was the first to be introduced to him and asked, 'How does your wife like having a police dog at home?' Holman replied that his wife was very fond of the dog. The Queen then asked how the dog got on with the children. Holman answered that they got on very well together. The

King, on the other hand, was a little more straightforward. 'You have a very good-looking dog. I shouldn't like him after me.'

The Royal command performance for Rex was followed shortly after by a demonstration of working service dogs for visiting officers of the French Navy at Imber Court. But perhaps Rex's most important demonstration had happened a few months before this, at the end of 1951.

Holman and Rex were asked to attend Imber Court for a special demonstration. There were two police officers there, Holman and Terry Shelton, who had a dog called Ben. They were then joined by PC Roberts with his dog Roger, and PC Elliott with Olly. Once there, they were told that the purpose of the display was to discover whether the dogs could be used to track bandits in Malaya.

At this time, the British Forces were engaged in jungle skirmishes with Malayan Bandits in an ongoing battle for independence. Included in the watching spectators that day were armed services, police and civilian top brass. Among the dignitaries were Colonel Young, Commissioner of the City of London Police, who was to go to Malaya. Also present were Herbert Dale from the Colonial Office and Sir Clive Latham, chairman of the Dunlop Rubber Company, who were particularly hit by the skirmishes as their rubber plantations were targeted.

There were demonstrations of general obedience tests, and then they moved to the woods between Esher and Oxshot, an overgrown wilderness of trees, bushes, and bracken, similar to the terrain of Malaya. Several officers had hidden themselves in the vastness of the dark woods and the dogs were charged with finding them. The spectators gathered on high ground to give them a wide, cinematic view of the area.

Rex and Holman went in first. Rex was undismayed by the tangle of undergrowth and ran straight into it to begin his search, the umbrella of low foliage blotting out daylight so that it was dark as night. Holman could not see where he was going as he followed his dog, and despite Rex having a cat's ability to see in the dark, he was compelled to search by air scent. In effect, he would be following any scent he could pick up, which is asking a great deal of any dog.

Eventually, Holman heard Rex calling, his barking muffled both by the undergrowth and the distance. Holman followed his dog, scrambling through the matted bushes and thorny ferns, until he found one Inspector Mount, chief trainer at Imber Court, cornered in the branches of a tree. Holman marched the prisoner to the hill where the audience was gathered.

Then it was Ben's turn, and he, too, found a bandit. Rex went away for a second time, discovering a man hiding in a hole at the side of a sand pit. Following the solo displays, Rex and Ben had to track two bandits who had run into the woods. It was some distance in before the trail divided, the bandits having gone in separate directions to the left and right.

Rex concentrated on one scent automatically, as did Ben, and they went in their opposite directions. The party on the top of the hill were watching as closely as they could as Rex tracked through the woods, reached a road, ran up it and branched off through a hedge. Holman couldn't understand this, as the dog had now taken him on a roundabout route towards the spectators. However, Rex went straight to a member of the audience who laughingly admitted that he was the man who had set the trail. Ben also caught his man and after Roger and Olly performed a similar seek, they returned to Imber Court where their handlers were questioned by VIPs on various aspects of dog handling.

In this way, they became the dogs who provided the template for training military dogs in the Malayan jungle during the conflagration there, and the template for subsequent armed service dog training.

Star Status, But Business As Usual

REX'S REPUTATION over the past few years had spread so much that he would soon become a film star. The film 'Police Dog', made in 1955, is not worth watching in its own right, but its saving grace is that it does contain the only film that exists of Rex III, even though the action that takes place within it is staged rather than real. This makes it invaluable as before TV and social media, only news reels might, if lucky, record the exploits of such a remarkable animal. However, before this celluloid adventure happened, Rex had another outing where he outwitted both the criminal and the officers searching for them.

It was another 4:30am call, but this time Holman was astounded to find a policeman outside who said, 'I've called two other dog handlers, and they've refused to come. They say they're not on call. I know you're not, but will you do the job?' Holman was astonished. He had never refused a call and couldn't believe that another dog handler would do this.

His reasoning was simple: when he became a dog handler, he accepted from the outset that he'd need to be on call at all hours of the day or night. So long as he was at home when the patrol car came, then he would answer the call. He had no hesitation in agreeing to the policeman's request and collecting Rex they sped to the scene of the crime, a building situated several miles away.

The first person he met was actually a former colleague

of his, from the Ghost Squad, whose face was covered with blood. When Holman asked what had happened, he was told that the man was the wireless operator of a radio car. At 3.07, they'd had a message from Scotland Yard reporting thieves in a warehouse. Their car rushed to the scene, where a Nightwatchman told them how he'd seen two men run from the offices and vanish into the dark. Sensibly knowing that he'd be no match for two men, the old fellow had dialled 999. When they arrived, the Nightwatchman joined the officers in combing the factory grounds, as he knew the lay of the land.

The wireless operator had spotted one of the thieves making his way towards a high fence. He had raced after him, but the crook had reached a fence and was scaling it. He was almost at the top of the fence when he had been grabbed by the wireless operator. The thief had kicked savagely down and caught the ex-Ghost Squad man in the face.

As he fell back, the thief dropped over the other side of the fence and splashed away across the shallows of the nearby river Wandle. A second crook had been grabbed as he entered the river by the second policeman. But after a struggle in the shallows, he also broke away and ran off with his accomplice.

By this time, more police cars had arrived and a thorough search was made of the area, both around the factory and also inside - after all, it was a possibility that, trying to be clever, they may have doubled back on their tracks and hidden in the warehouse until the fuss died down. Someone had suggested calling a dog, and Holman and Rex had arrived two hours after the event, with much of that time having been lost in the visits to handlers who turned it down.

When Holman entered the factory, he was asked by the Inspector in charge, 'Do you think it's any good after all this time? I expect they've got away.'

Holman was used to this, as we've seen. He replied, 'Well, since I've been pulled cold from my bed, I might as well have a look. Apart from anything else, I feel a bit strongly about this because I don't like policemen being kicked in the face.'

Holman took Rex into the factory. 'Find him,' he urged. Without any hesitation, Rex dashed to the far end of the building and circled around the base of a large, 20-foot-high water tank, barking and leaping. Holman asked if anyone had looked in the tank. 'There's nobody up there,' he was told, 'we've all had a look.' Holman thought it unlikely that every officer there had been up the side of the tank but saw their point. Still... 'Rex says you're wrong,' he said flatly. 'I'll take a look.'

There was a ladder propped against the wall of the factory. Holman took it to the tank and shinned up. Inside, soaking wet, were two youths. Rex had taken 30 seconds to do something a posse of policemen had failed to do in two hours. 'Don't make any trouble,' Holman said, 'or I'll send the dog after you, and he can climb ladders.'

They came down quietly. In questioning they admitted they had doubled back to the factory and since they were both already soaking wet after the river and running through the rain, they felt they couldn't get any wetter. So, they may as well try hiding in the tank. When they'd heard someone mount the ladder to examine the inside, they pressed themselves close against the sides. In so doing, they kept themselves underneath the officer's line of vision when he looked over the top.

They were charged, and at the quarter sessions they were sentenced for 12 months. Holman did not need to attend, as evidence of arrest was given by a constable, who described Rex's tracking of the criminals as fantastic. The judge jokingly suggested that Rex III should be made District Commissioner of Police Dogs for this display of his remarkable talents. 'If the dog is ever in this vicinity while I'm in court, I should like to see him,' the judge added.

Not long after this, in October of 1953, Superintendent Peck of the dog section asked Holman to attend Scotland Yard. The reason was not given. So, Holman was rather confused when he turned up at the Yard. However, whatever he had suspected, he did not expect what Peck asked, 'Do you think Rex could be trained to detect drugs?'

Holman replied that he didn't know for sure, but he couldn't see why not. Peck handed him two packages. Each had a different type of dope in it. He added that two other dogs had been tried, and both had failed. Holman said he'd give Rex a try. Peck gave him a month to do this, adding that this was top secret. 'Do the training in your own time.'

Later that day, when Holman was at home wondering how best to train Rex, his wife was inspired to remark that if he took some of it himself, it might give him the inspiration he was looking for. It was a joke, but it did provide him with an idea for training.

He started the course in his own house: he held the drugs under the dog's nose so that he could get the not very strong scent, then he had small quantities of the stuff he placed on the floor and said 'Dope. Fetch it.' It took time, but Rex came to understand that when the order fetch was prefaced by dope, he was only to look for items bearing either or both of the smells to which he was being introduced. Holman tried him on one type first, then the other, and then mixed them.

Eventually he was able to omit 'Fetch' and just use the word 'Dope', which was enough to send Rex searching under cushions, round chairs, and on top of tables. It wasn't the easiest of tasks for the dog as the small packets were very hard to detect, but he did master it.

In terms of this 'dope', it should be noted that the kind of drugs available back in the 1950s had a much more subtle scent than those on the streets today, which no dog would have any trouble detecting.

Home training came to an end when he knocked over a vase of flowers. 'I don't mind his paws on the furniture,' Holman's wife told him, 'But I do object to him spilling flowers and water on the floor.' There was no doubt in Holman's mind that she blamed him for this, and not her Rexy.

Now, Holman moved the training to the gymnasium at the police station and the Alsatian's nose became so acute that he could sniff a thimbleful of dope when it was well hidden out of sight. Getting at it, Rex would inform Holman of its presence with barks and leaps. There was a fortnight of intensive training indoors and on the common at Mitcham. Scope was broadened to include detection when hidden on a person's body. Again, the amount was small. No more than would be used for a single 'reefer', as they were called at that time.

Moving back into the house – when his wife wasn't there – Holman used his son, Richard, as a guinea pig. He hid a small quantity of dope in the sleeve of his son's shirt, brought Rex into the room, and said 'Dope'. The dog searched the furniture, walls, floor, and finding nothing came back, looking plainly baffled. Holman repeated the order.

Suddenly, Rex gave Richard a passing sniff, stopped dead, and barked. He made no attempt to worry at him but sniffed at him until he discovered where the tiny package was hidden, trying to work it from the shirt sleeve with his nose. Holman went further and hid drugs in his wife and daughter's handbags, and Rex found them despite the scent being overwhelmed by face powder and perfume.

Holman's next move was to get half a dozen male cleaners at the police station to go to the gym, in their lunch break, to help train Rex in finding – as they thought – small objects. They were agreeable and he hid some of the dope under the collar of one cleaner's jacket, lined them up, then whispered the order to the dog because he didn't want them to hear the word 'dope'. After a quick search, Rex found it.

The cleaners enjoyed this, and the exercise went on for a week. Holman varied it as much as he could, hiding it either on a cleaner in the gym, more than one cleaner, in more than one place, and so forth. The final test, which Rex passed without trouble, was to hide packages in various rooms at the police station and get him to search for them.

In November, he presented Rex at Scotland Yard. Apart from the senior officers present there were also a number of men from the narcotics section of the Home Office. Rex's first task was to find a reefer hidden somewhere in the office next to them. Given the order, Rex bounded into the neighbouring room and immediately perched on a desk, his nose in a typewriter, frustrated as he couldn't get at what he was sniffing. He barked, and Holman discovered the reefer hidden in the machine's roller. In another room, the dope had been hidden in a suitcase, in a cupboard, and smaller quantities concealed in various other places around the building. Rex found all of it quickly.

When the last package was sniffed and recovered, the senior home office man turned to Peck and asked when he could take Holman and Rex off duty, as he wanted them seconded to him straight away. He added, 'You saw me time him. When the dope was hidden in the cupboard, it took just under five minutes. It would have taken my men more than half an hour to have emptied all those drawers and cupboards. Think of the manpower savings.'

Rex's pioneering work as the first dog to be trained for drug sniffing in the UK became part of a training program that all other forces undertook. One amusing sideline came when a party of police officers arrived from the West Indies to train and become handlers for dope seeking dogs, which they were to take back to the Caribbean. They brought their own dope with them and were promptly detained by the customs at Liverpool. They explained that they had brought it with them as they wanted to make sure the dogs would recognise the dope they had prevalent in the Islands. The customs officers were amused, and replied that police or not, you can't smuggle dope into the country. So, these unfortunate officers spent a few hours in custody before phone calls to Scotland Yard smoothed things over.

Lights. Camera. Action?

REX'S TIME on the cinema screens of Britain was about to come knocking: it was while the drug training was going on that Holman was contacted from Scotland Yard and told to report to the Keston dog training centre. Keston, down in Kent, had only just recently taken over from Imber Court as a newer facility for Met dog training. Down at Keston, Holman had to report to Chief Inspector Matthews, the officer in charge. There he met Harold Houth, a producer, and director Derek Twist. Also present was the superintendent from Scotland Yard, who had called Holman down. Houth and Twist had a notion to put a real police dog in their planned film 'Police Dog', and they believed the ideal dog for them would be Rex, as he had set the highest standards.

Rex was prepared and had to have some sample film taken. In essence, he had to have a screen test. Of course, he passed easily. Perhaps the idea was to emulate the success of Rin Tin Tin, a former US police dog who had been the hero of a number of silent thriller films, and was once the most famous film star in the world. He, too, had been an Alsatian. Holman was not convinced, as his memoirs show, and this was only reinforced when the script was delivered to him. The human stars of the film were Joan Rice, Tim Turner, Sandra Dorne and Charles Victor, with a credit 'Introducing Rex III, the hero of 90 arrests'.

The story was a fairly standard crime plot, with Turner as Rex's handler, and involves a love story, a girl gone bad, and the dog saving the day. It runs as follows: Constables Mason (Turner) and Lade spot a burglar leaving the scene of the crime and both give chase. Lade is shot and badly wounded by the burglar before Mason can catch up with him. Later, back at the police station Mason befriends Rex, a stray Alsatian dog recently brought in by another officer. Its owners have moved abroad, and on being contacted they agree to donate it to the police.

Rex and Mason begin training together, causing tensions back home with Mason's girlfriend Pat Lewis. She is his land-lady's daughter. Her late father was also a policeman, but she acts towards Mason as if she knows nothing of what being a policeman means. She resents being unable to treat Rex as a pet, and the fact the dog is drawing Mason's attention away from their relationship. Rex and Mason complete their training and go on patrol on the streets of Hampstead. Meanwhile, Lade has died from his injuries and his killer continues to lie low, taking on temporary work as a builder's labourer until the CID arrives and he is forced to flee. Throughout this, Mason and

Pat's relationship becomes more and more strained, and he decides to move out, along with Rex. Soon afterwards, they are deployed to a factory where Lade's killer is breaking into a safe. They pursue him, with Rex holding onto the killer long enough to make an arrest. Meaning to meet Mason for a final discussion about their relationship, Pat arrives at the crime scene and instead reconciles with both Mason and Rex.

Reading it, aside from seeing how poor it was as a story, and how unlike the real Rex, Holman could see that the main issue for him would be that Rex would have to walk with Tim Turner.

Now, Rex would not walk to heel with anyone except Holman, and he would not take orders from anyone except Holman. So, the problem was how to get him to go with Turner. For these shots, Holman tried using a lead and practising with his son Richard, who would walk with Rex on the lead while Holman waited. But Rex did not like the idea and kept looking back to where Holman was standing.

Then, Rex met Tim Turner at the studio and allowed him to stroke and pet him, as Turner was in police uniform. But as soon as Holman moved away, the dog trotted after him. To overcome this, Holman suggested that they have Rex on a lead – as he had tried with Richard - and had Turner trying to act like he was still training the dog this way. Rex would then walk with him, but only if he was sent to the end of a road, turned round, and could see Holman waiting for him. The film would then be shot silently, so that Holman could give the command and Rex would walk towards him, allowing Turner to take him on the lead.

If you can get to see the film, in one scene Rex has to dig his way out of a coal cellar, and Holman achieved this effect by burying a parcel in some coal and commanding Rex to fetch. By photographing this from behind, the impression was created not that he was digging his way into the coal, but out of the cellar. They then completed the scene by filming Rex coming through the cellar flaps. Apparently, Rex played this flawlessly, but he had to be re-shot because they forgot to put film in one of the cameras... Holman was frustrated by how wasteful the rehearsals and endless retakes were. After a couple of run throughs, Rex knew exactly what to do and it was the human actors that would let him down.

Holman was teased by his colleagues about the venture into films, and they were surprised when he told them truthfully that he'd not received a penny out of the production. It was all part of a day's duty for Rex, albeit not the run of the mill duty.

There are only a few reviews of the film that can be found from the time. 'Picture Goer' said: 'An agreeable and occasionally thrilling "Blue Lamp" style melodrama. It's a pat on the back for police dogs. The human players do not count for much, but Rex III the famous police dog has his day.'

'The Monthly Film Bulletin' wrote: 'Artlessly and unpretentiously made, this is a mildly pleasing little thriller. Its main attraction – particularly for young audiences – is the dog star, and the illustration of the methods used in training him.'

'Kine Weekly' added: 'The picture, although made with the full co-operation of the authorities, fails fully to convince, but at least it ends in exciting style. The plot is nothing to shout about, and the same goes for the acting, but the four-footed star, Rex III, who incidentally has a fine record, is shrewdly exploited and prevents any serious flagging. Joan Rice has little to do as Pat, Tim Turner lacks experience as Frank, and Cecil Brock and Sandra Dorne fall short of demands as the killer and his moll respectively. The rest of the humans are equally transparent, but Rex undoubtedly does his stuff. In a word, the film is made, or, rather, saved by the pooch.'

The film may not have endured, but the coverage at the time, like the reprinted for decades 'Look And Learn' strip, imprinted Rex as the image of a police dog for generations. And not just with the public: having recalled from my primary school days the police dog handled by the father of a friend, it's worth mentioning that he was an Alsatian called Rex…

Curtain Call…

MEANWHILE, IT was back to business as usual. Another night call-out, to Stratton Hill Theatre at 2:30am on a Friday. Holman and Rex arrived to help search for two men seen on the roof. Rex was up the fire escape ahead of Holman. It was a long climb, and at the top Holman's torch picked out the dog some yards ahead, sniffing along the edge of the parapet and proceeding more slowly and cautiously than usual.

Looking over, Holman could see that they were high up with a long drop down from the narrow parapet. He called Rex back and said to the Inspector who had followed him up, 'Look how high we are. Look at the drop. If he slips over the side in the darkness, he'll be killed. And I'm not risking my dog's life for a couple of thieves. Have you looked inside the theatre?'

The Inspector replied that they had, and there was no one in there. The two men were seen on the roof trying to get in, so they must have escaped the same way. Holman understood this, but was still unconvinced about the risk. He decided to search inside the building regardless, before taking a chance he did not think necessary. He took the dog into the theatre and ordered 'Find'.

Rex looked through the stalls and boxes, found nothing, and

then just when Holman thought they were wasting their time, with a bark Rex jumped to the side of the stage and dashed towards one of the heavy stage curtains. The two men were hiding in there; they'd had the nerve to break into the theatre and hide at the side of the stage, avoiding detection when it was searched. They were hoping to carry out their robbery of the manager's office when the police left the building. Rex had other ideas.

Courage In The Face Of Death

SHORTLY AFTER this, on June 13th, 1954, they were on duty during the day, and it was raining heavily when Holman booked in at the police station before taking Rex out on patrol. By 11:15 they returned, back to the station, where Holman dried Rex off before they went to the canteen. While they were there, a CID sergeant came up and told Holman he was going to pick up an Army deserter in Tynemouth Road – would Rex and Holman like to tag along and watch the back of the house in case he tried to make a run for it?

Holman agreed, and when they reached Tynemouth Road, he went to the back with Rex and waited for something to happen. Usually, these assignments were a brief knock at the door, introductions, a search, maybe a scuffle, a formal caution, and within five minutes they were on the way back to the police station.

This time, 10 minutes had passed with no indication of anything happening. Waiting, Holman realised that if something was going on he wouldn't know the name of the man they were after, or his description. He would have to stop anyone who came out the back. After 20 minutes, still nothing had happened. Holman decided to take Rex round to the front and find out what was causing a delay.

As they reached the front, they could hear shouting, and a man broke away from the police car. He ran around a corner and into Ashburn Road. Holman yelled a command, and Rex was away. Holman sprinted after him and saw Rex turn down Ashburn Road. As he cornered, he saw the man, still running, thrust his hand into the pockets of his raincoat and pull out a gun. Without slowing, he half-turned, took aim and fired. Mercifully, he missed Rex, and as he pulled the trigger, Rex leapt up and sank his teeth into the gunman's right arm. As he tried to shake free and moved his arm to do so, the revolver was fired a second time.

As this was fired, Holman's attention was so firmly upon Rex and the gunman that he didn't see the low wall projecting from the corner of the houses, tripping over it and tumbling headlong onto the pavement. A constable following behind rushed past and made for the gunman, grabbing him. Rex still had his grip on the gunman's arm, relaxed only when the constable arrived. But when the constable hesitated for a moment, seemingly afraid of the dog, the gunman saw his chance and pulled away.

Rex had started to run back to Holman, having released, and did not at first see the gunman pull free and start to run back towards him, hoping to get past the dog and Holman, who was still on the pavement. Holman called out, and Rex responded: he whirled round and headed back for the gunman, who stopped and with brutal deliberation levelled the gun. He held back until Rex was about to leap and then pushed the revolver into the dog's face and pulled the trigger...

There was a loud explosion. Rex spun in a complete circle and fell to the ground, motionless and silent. Holman was too numb to feel anything: how could the man have missed?

By stopping to shoot at the dog, the gunman lost a valuable couple of seconds, allowing the constable to grab hold of him again. Holman's immediate concern was for the dog and as he went forward, he saw the gunman struggling grimly with the policeman. But before he could reach Rex, to his absolute amazement and delight, Rex trembled, raised his head, and climbed to his feet. He was obviously dazed and couldn't see, yet such was his courage and devotion to duty that he began to stagger towards the sound of the scuffle.

'Down,' Holman commanded as he knelt beside his dog. He could see that the bullet had grazed the dog's left ear, and that his eyes were blinded by white spots of powder burns. With a whimper, he sat there trying to paw away the pain in his eyes. Holman left him for a moment and helped the constable subdue the gunman.

After they had forced him into the patrol car, the CID sergeant said, 'Good job we took you with us this morning – he'd have got away if it hadn't been for Rex'. Holman didn't quite feel this way as the police car took him home. He carried Rex indoors. He told his wife briefly what had happened, and she stood silently as he bathed the Alsatian's eyes and ear with boracic crystals dissolved in warm water. After a while, he could tell that Rex was able to see again, so he felt a little better.

He took Rex to the police vet, where the dog was not even responsive to the vet he loathed, showing how shocked he was. The police vet told Holman that the burn marks would disappear within a few days, leaving no permanent injury. With this, the fear vanished from Holman's mind. Rex constantly wiped his eyes that day with his paws and was obviously in pain.

Holman's wife and daughter took turns at bathing Rex's

eyes, and a procession of press photographers came to the house during the afternoon, asking for permission to take pictures. When he took Rex for his run, Holman went down the streets along which they chased the gunman in the hope of finding witnesses, and some photographs were taken along that route.

Rex was due to take part in a display the next day. Rex's sight seemed to be perfect, despite the ugly white spots, and much of the pain seemed to have gone. So, Holman did not withdraw. However, the display did include a gun chase, and he wondered whether it was advisable to subject Rex to this so soon after his real shooting. On reflection, he decided that he would not cancel the chase. As with a lot of post-action scenarios, he decided it would enable him to see whether the dog's nerve had been affected by the experience, and if he was still responsive.

Considering how Rex had climbed to his feet and staggered blindly towards the gunman when wounded, Holman should have known better than to question Rex's courage. Despite blank cartridges being fired from close range, Rex took down his assailant without faltering. If anything, it made him more savage, and Chief Inspector Matthews, the target man, found that his suit was well beyond repair by the time the dog had finished with him. Filled with pride, Holman swept Rex into his arms as he carried him off the field.

While this was going on, the CID Sergeant gave evidence against the gunman at Southwestern Magistrates Court, and Mr. Clyde Wilson's first words were 'How is Rex?'

The CID man, the Constable and Holman were awarded 15 pounds from the Bow Street reward fund. Ironically, when Holman went to receive his award, he had to leave Rex behind: the only occasion during his time with Rex was when he went on duty without him. After the award had been made, both Holman and his wife were impatient to get home - his wife, because he promised to buy her a gold watch with the reward, and Holman because he didn't like Rex being left alone.

At the Old Bailey, the gunman received 12 years imprisonment, while the press reports resulted in more fan mail for Rex. A medal came from a group of Mitcham residents, engraved 'To Rex III, for his courage and devotion to duty'. Some weeks after, Holman had to attend Tooting police station at two o'clock one afternoon, and his wife was asked to go with him. Rex was awarded with two medals in recognition of his tackling the gunman: the PDSA silver medal, presented by Lord Amwell, and the National Canine Defence League medal, presented by Mr. Neve. This was only the second medal for bravery awarded by the PDSA, the other having been given to a dog in Manchester for saving lives during a fire.

It was also the first time a police dog would be presented with any sort of medal for bravery. Another piece of history for Rex. He had made 125 arrests during his career. After 1954, these arrests had slowed down for no other reason than that his success had led to an enlargement of the dog section. This meant that other dogs were now in action and making arrests. The weight of being so successful was now off Rex, and he was heading towards his last couple of working years before retirement.

A Sudden Shock

SADLY, THIS was not to be. In May 1956, Rex developed a cough and began to suck air noisily through his nose. It was the first time he'd shown any sign of any illness. Was it somehow connected with the trauma he had suffered from the gunshot wound? It's impossible to know. Rex kept coughing for the next ten days. His coat became dull, which it never had before, and his reactions were blunted compared to previously. Holman called the dog training centre at Keston and asked if he could bring Rex to the police vet.

At first, they thought it was no more than sore tonsils. But his illness continued, even after Holman had painted his throat with lotion several times a day for a fortnight. His continuing illness meant that x-rays were taken. It was discovered that Rex had a tumour in his throat, and it was possibly an inoperable cancer.

Holman was heartbroken by this. Rex had exploratory surgery to see if there was any hope, but it was discovered to be a large throat cancer. There was no chance of surgery to save him.

Holman took Rex to Keston to have him put to sleep. Holman and Rex were picked up by van and taken to Keston, just as they had been picked up when they were first paired and travelled to Imber Court.

On arrival at Keston, Holman could not face seeing Rex taken in this way and asked a Sergeant Murphy to take Rex into the vet for euthanasia. His last act was to pat Rex on his head and stroke his ear, telling him was a good dog, and to stay as he moved away. The last he saw was Rex sitting, obeying the word of the handler who was more than that: they were a team, and Holman loved that dog.

Rex was the first police dog to make people really aware of what dogs could do for the service and for the public. He was an incredible animal and had a charisma worthy of his fame. More than that, he was his handler's best friend and partner.

Rex was euthanised and buried in the woods at Keston. Holman didn't know where and didn't want to know where. He did have other police dogs after Rex, but none were ever the same.

Holman wrote that when he died something vital went out of him. 'For in Rex, I really did give my heart to a dog to tear.'

Police Constable Alan Beddoe of the British Transport police with his dog Major the German Shepherd in Cardiff in March, 1983

PART THREE 🐾🐾🐾
Late 20th Century Police Work

Major: The Quarry, The Thief And The Wardrobe

The Dog That Wouldn't Move

INSPECTOR TONY Kitts stood on the pavement outside the house in Penarth Road and looked at the dog in front of him. A black and tan, long haired German Shepherd, Kitts had recognised him immediately.

'Look, old son, I know you're only supposed to answer to your handler, but you can't sit here all night making a show of yourself, can you?' he said. The dog didn't seem to be listening, staring straight ahead at the front door of the house.

Aware that he was just talking to himself, Kitts murmured, 'What I'd like to know is how you got here, and just what's behind that door that you won't move...'

The Pioneers Who Were Almost Left Behind

THE BRITISH Transport Police have officers who do not use dogs, just as they had back in the days when they were separate Docks and Rail forces in the Victorian and Edwardian era. But it has to be said that the introduction of dogs changed the whole manner in which the transport police viewed themselves and the way in which they carried out their duties. They became a force where the use of a dog was a pre-eminent and vital part of their planning and procedure. It was not all plain sailing, and later developments looked to throw away the hard work of the pioneering officers.

Last seen, Inspector Herbert Shelton had replaced the retiring Inspector John Morrell and sought to take his work one step further, overseeing the construction of a new training centre which was now based at Elstree, in Hertfordshire. This meant that a larger number of dogs could now be trained and dog handler posts were established at many stations and docks around the country which had not as yet been 'manned' by a dog.

One of these was Southampton docks, which formed its dog section in 1962. It was 11 years after this that Constable 'Spud' Murphy trained his general-purpose dog to detect cannabis. His Superintendent was so impressed by this that he then obtained a dog named Cap who was used specifically for this purpose. The use of specific sniffer dogs for drugs, although growing in use, was still not widespread and so the introduction of such a valuable tool was not to be sniffed at (groan).

It is an anomaly when it comes to dock and port working that although the BTP have authority over the actual dock area, the ships that come into dock do not fall under their purview, and it is the County Constabulary and City Forces who are called upon to search these ships when required.

After all, smuggling as a criminal enterprise has never gone away, and drugs, cash, guns, and ammunition can all be safely stowed in secret on a ship, leaving the smuggler with only the problem of getting from ship to shore undetected.

This is where co-operation between the BTP and local forces

comes into operation, and the sniffer dog from land can take to the water.

The Overlooked Heroes

THE BRITISH Transport Police tend to be overlooked by the public in the light of other forces, simply because their work does not happen on the streets where most people would notice. Nonetheless, the bravery and courage shown by these dogs and their handlers is well worth recording.

A perfect example of this happened the year after Murphy had his drug dog breakthrough. In July of 1974, PC Don Gordon was out with his dog when they came across a man stealing cable from the Grand Terminus Junction, Glasgow. Gordon's dog was named Jim, following in the tradition of one of those first four Airedales, though as with the prevailing trends, this Jim was an Alsatian. The Junction itself is long closed now and much of it has been redeveloped into housing, but at that time it served as part of the Glasgow Harbour Railway, which had opened in the 1840s to serve the quays and docks from the coalfields of Lanarkshire. By the 1980s the last vestiges of any goods and services along the Harbour Railway had dwindled, and closure had started.

In the 1970s, there was still enough trade in the dock to warrant a patrol, and PC Gordon was alone in dockland which was run down and deserted by day, and almost desolate by night. It was not a safe, easy route, but no BTP copper signs up for a holiday.

Gordon and Jim came across a thief who felt that it would be a simple enough job to gather up a reel of cable and cross the deserted tracks, reach the boundary wall, get through it, and take his haul to a waiting fence. An easy night's work. It might have been, if not for Gordon and Jim. Yelling at him and setting the dog free, Gordon approached the thief, who left the cable and produced a knife. Gordon closed in on him, and was slashed in the face for his trouble. Face covered in blood, he staggered back, and Jim moved in. The dog went for the man's arm as trained, and was stabbed in the side. He pulled back yelping, as much in shock as pain. Leaving his haul behind him, the thief took advantage of what he thought was their incapacity, and made for the boundary.

He reckoned with the tenacity and courage of both dog and handler. Gordon ran after his assailant, wiping blood from his face, adrenaline kicking in and blanking the pain he might otherwise feel. The same was true for Jim, who followed his handler and stuck to his duty. They chased after their assailant across the tracks and brought him down. He was a desperate man, and still had his knife. He had no hesitation in striking out again, inflicting further wounds on Gordon and on Jim. But they did not stop: working together as a team, Gordon disarmed the man and cuffed him while Jim secured him as trained, jaws clamped to his arm, ignoring the knife as it struck at him again.

After they had taken him in, Gordon required 38 stitches to wounds received, while Jim needed veterinary attention. Fortunately for both man and dog, the wounds were not serious. Both Gordon and Jim were recipients of the Whitbread Shield. This was presented to the BTP in 1966 by Mr RJ Whitbread and is for "meritorious police work not within other spheres of the service such as gallantry or dedicated First Aid work". It was intended to be an annual award but in fact was only presented 15 times during its 45-year history (it was discontinued in 2011, and the last award was 2006). This was the only time that it was ever presented to both a handler and his dog.

Moving ahead to 1989, the Lockerbie Air Disaster occurred on December 21st when a bomb exploded on a passenger jet as it passed over the village. It was actually two BTP dog handlers, Davy Connell and Alastair Campbell, who were first on the scene. Using the dogs to track in the wreckage, they began the thankless task of attempting to recover the bodies of the passengers, and to search in the vain hope of finding survivors. The dogs uncovered 23 bodies during a 33-hour shift. At the end of this, two further handlers - Callum Weir and Neil Russell - and their dogs began a shift that saw them remain on site combing wreckage until the end of the search, four weeks later.

In more recent years, when suicide bombers attacked the London Underground on July 7th, 2005, it was the BTP who were instrumental in the search for any further explosives using the Explosive Search Dogs - sniffers trained specifically for any explosive substances - that had recently been trained and called into service.

Vinnie, a search dog handled by PC Dave Coleman, searched the Kings Cross site prior to bodies being removed, their brief to locate any survivors not yet evacuated, and to search for any sign of further danger before crews moved in for clearance. A search dog named Ross was called from the BTP to assist the Met in searching the site of the bus explosion in Tavistock Square - both the bus itself and surrounding area - for secondary devices, securing the site for the Met to move in.

Not All Plain Sailing...

YOU MIGHT think that with such a distinguished record, the achievements of the dog section within the BTP would enable them to grow unfettered, however this could not be further from the truth. At the time that Don Gordon and Jim were risking their lives and winning awards for their courage and devotion to duty, the BTP had a new Chief Constable, Eric Haslam, who had joined from the Kent County Constabulary. He took one look at the record of dog handlers, who had an arrest count of 738 in 1973, rising to 908 in 1974 – the year of Gordon and Jim – and his reaction to such good work was to reduce the dog section to 22 officers. The following year he cut the budget even more, and closed the Elstree Dog Training School at the end of 1975. This reduced the number of dogs from 52 to 22.

Thankfully, all Chief Constables have to retire at some point, and Haslam's successors saw more worth in the dog section and the history it had forged. The budget was restored and increased to bring the section back up to speed. After Elstree was closed, training was moved to Tadworth, and then in 2010 the training school was moved again, this time to Keston where it shares with the Met Police. The irony that after Haslam's cuts the training school eventually ended up located in a centre that was inspired by Hedon Hall and Elstree should not be lost...

Currently, the BTP dog section has 64 dogs, with handlers often having more than one dog. There are 22 general purpose dogs, six drug detection dogs, and 34 explosive detection dogs. Such is their cachet that BTP handlers are often called upon by other forces to perform duties away from the railways and transport systems that gave them their name.

But this does not mean that they are safe. At a time when costs increase and budgets allotted to police forces are squeezed ever tighter, the dog section will always be the first to come under scrutiny for costs.

This is understandable to a degree. You buy a piece of equipment and that is your only cost until it needs replacement. Maintenance on most equipment is low. Dogs, on the other hand, are relatively high maintenance. They need to be housed and fed; there are vet bills; their useful life as 'equipment' is not predictable as injury or illness can cut this short unexpectedly. The police still see the dog as a 'tool', and when considered as such they can be pretty expensive ones. If you're looking to cut costs and get the maximum bang for your buck, then a dog is probably not going to be top of your list.

Yet time and again dogs have proved themselves in the field to be effective and many times faster than a man. When Rex III, the first dog trained to detect drugs, was introduced over seven decades ago, a Customs and Excise man remarked that he was able to find drugs faster and with less manpower than a conventional search. That was then: nothing has changed since, and a dog can still effect a search faster than a number of officers. And it was a BTP dog whose tenacity and persistence led to a quite remarkable piece of police work. Many of the places in which these dogs worked were now in decline, but the job was still paramount.

A Dying Area

FOR THE British Transport Police, the 1970s and 1980s were times of radical change in their duties. They had always been at the forefront of using dogs, even if their successes were out of the public eye and their training schools had not gained the same cachet as Surrey's Mount Browne. Nonetheless, they had been the model for the advances of Surrey and the Met, and their dogs were some of the most successful in the field.

Their problem – in other sections as well as the dog section – was that there was a shift in what they were required to do. Their origins, as we have seen, lay in the rail companies who serviced the docks, and their initial work had been focused on the ports and dockyards of the UK. Those ports and docks were in decline. Goods and services came by road and by air now, and although British Rail still conveyed goods and containers, as they do today, these were now picked up from sites other than the port.

As a result, the docks were in decline. The Port of London Authority now focused most of its attention at Tilbury, the East End Docklands lying empty and derelict.

Some ports and docks survived, but they were a shadow of their former selves: now empty and falling into disrepair, they were places of shadow and silence, even by day. There were still pickings for the criminal fraternity from the businesses that remained, and accessing them was now much easier. For the BTP patrols, work was harder as they were working in areas that had derelict buildings and wharves, with plenty of places to be ambushed or to fall prey to rotting wood and loose brickwork.

There was more danger: this was demonstrated by the previously mentioned events at Glasgow Terminus Junction, when PC Don Gordon and PD Jim sustained injuries while making an arrest. In the quiet of the derelict dock and rail yard, a patrol had to tread with care.

Cardiff was faring little better than Glasgow at this time: both locations had areas that were still working docks, but much of the old dockyard was falling into wasteland. Presently, the Cardiff Harbour Authority has three docks which are still in use; the rest were already dead by the time that the 1980s had come round.

The dock area of Cardiff had been known as Tiger Bay since Victorian times, and the name had become a synonym for any dock area around the globe that had a population pressed tightly together, trying to survive in poverty. The original Tiger

Bay is famous for two things: the high level of crime, and for producing Shirley Bassey, the vocalist whose talent carried her out of the slums in the 1950s and 60s. Anyone who has ever seen a biopic or documentary about her will have some indication of the conditions she was born into. These conditions had lessened by the turn of the 1980s only in so much as the population was falling as people moved out in search of work. The housing had always been poor and on the edge of dereliction. Now it was falling apart from neglect and the number of properties that were now empty. Boarded up windows, closed shops, and a population that was described as one of the most deprived in Wales.

It was no wonder, then, that there was always some kind of criminal activity to occupy the local police…

A Safe Use Of A Forklift...

AT THE start of 1983 there had been a spate of crimes around the dock area that the BTP CID believed to be connected. A series of offences, mostly petty burglary and culminating in a car theft, had been centred around the Collingdon Road area. Now, this area has been redeveloped and has new housing and business that was funded by a regeneration scheme. Looking at recent photographs of it, it's hard to reconcile it with the area as it looked over four decades ago: the streets are virtually empty, the houses boarded up, with those few small factories and warehouses that remained open appearing as half-empty and half-closed. It was an area where it was easy to commit crime, even though the results yielded may be so poor as to make the criminal wonder why they took the risk.

CID had their usual list of suspects. In an area like the old Tiger Bay, the local faces soon become known, and their methods of working hardly ever vary. Police work is the same the world over: the odds are always in favour of it being a repeat offender who has passed through your hands at some point. In an area that was teetering on the edge of collapse and disappearing completely, it was a small pool with only a few fish.

But even they can spring a few surprises: the audacity of the latest raid on Collingdon Road was breathtaking. A small engineering works had been the target. They carried some cash from the everyday business as well as their payroll. This was kept in a safe in the office of the works. You would expect a break-in, and an attempt to crack or break the safe, under the cover of darkness while maintaining a low profile.

Not for these boys: they were going to hit hard, fast, and make a swift getaway. And it was obvious from their method of entry that they had no qualms about subterfuge or subtlety...

Their first task was to steal a forklift truck. In itself this was a minor, if baffling, theft. Why would they want such a vehicle, and where could they hope to sell it? Few if any businesses would want to buy a stolen vehicle of this type. But before CID had a chance to look into any aspect of this, the team that had stolen the forklift made their intentions plain.

The forklift truck was used to smash through the brickwork in the outer wall of the engineering shop, creating a hole large enough for the rest of the team to get through, then wrestle the safe from the office and towards the hole in the wall. The forklift was used to pick up the safe and transport it to a van, where it was stowed in the back and driven away at speed while the rest of the team dispersed, leaving the forklift in the middle of the street, and a gaping hole in the side of the engineering works.

Their reliance on speed rather than stealth proved a good call, as by the time the police were on the scene they were long gone, the safe with them, and the one area in which they had shown care was in making sure that there were no identifiable prints or traces of their identities on what was left behind.

A Quarry In A Quarry

INVESTIGATIONS WERE going nowhere. The BTP were responsible for covering the theft as the engineering works was on Port land, but they had also liaised with the Cardiff Police as the perpetrators could be anywhere in the city. So far, both CID teams had drawn a blank, and there were no leads to go on. Until they had a phone call out of the blue. The caller was a woman named Kate. She worked around the dock area and was well-known to police. When she told them she had information regarding the theft of the safe and its current whereabouts, CID assumed that she had picked up something from a customer, or from her regular haunts. What they didn't expect was that she would put the finger on her brother. He had been part of the robbery gang, and she knew from him where the safe had been stowed. She also knew that as yet this had not been broken or blown open. When asked why she would do this, she did not say: perhaps she had no love for her brother, or she was using whatever she knew to try and make a few pounds in reward, or both. Ultimately, it didn't matter. All that did matter was that the money was still in the safe, waiting for someone to come along and get it open...

Kate told the police that the safe had been stowed in a disused quarry in Leckwith, just outside Cardiff. Acting on this information, a team was dispatched to the quarry to hunt for it. Kate had been on the money – literally – for the safe was found hidden in the overgrown quarry. Calling in, the team wanted to arrange removal, but the officer in charge – Inspector Vic

Miller – had other ideas. He felt sure that the perpetrators would return to the site to either open the safe, or remove it to where it could be opened. He asked the team if they were certain they had not been observed; if they had not, and he relied on Kate not letting slip that she had informed the police, then he was sure that at least some of the criminal gang would return to the safe.

All the police would have to do is wait…

Surveillance

MILLER LEFT the team that had discovered the safe in situ, and arranged surveillance teams to take over. He included himself, and also two dog handlers, as he felt dogs may be useful if anyone returning tried to make a run for it. The two handlers assigned were PC John Mellor and his dog, and PC Allan Beddoe, who handled a four-year-old black and tan long haired German Shepherd called Major.

It would be Major's tenacity and intelligence that would eventually prove decisive in the case, even if his actions initially seemed to be inexplicable.

It was light when they arrived and took up their positions. As the evening drew in – rapidly as it was still early in the year – and the air gained a chill, the surveillance team wondered how long they would have to wait. It was possible that it could be any number of days and nights before any of the perpetrators returned. Each man hidden in the darkness cursed and the cold and pondered how many nights of it there were in for. They settled themselves in, resigned to a long stretch.

It turned out that they wouldn't have to wait that long at all: as darkness enveloped the quarry, there were sounds coming over the still night air. They were faint, but they were voices, speaking in brief undertones. Then came the scrabbling, scratching sounds of pebbles and small rocks being dislodged and falling. It was hard to determine where around the quarry the sounds came from: a problem that was suddenly solved as one of two men stood up against the sky, on the edge of the rock face. A second man joined him. Even in the almost complete darkness they made no effort to hide, unaware and not even considering they were being watched.

As the surveillance team waited, each man unable to quite believe what he was seeing, the two men lowered themselves down the side of the quarry on ropes, before going across the floor of the pit to where the safe was hidden. Producing a heavy hammer and a crowbar, the two men started to methodically attack the safe, trying to break into it. They hammered at the back of the safe, trying to penetrate the metal, not bothering with the niceties of breaking the lock. They attacked the safe with no regard for the noise they made, swearing at each other in frustration as their efforts made little impression.

Obviously, they felt completely secure in not being seen or overheard in this location. Equally obviously, they were totally wrong…

The surveillance team had been observing them, not moving, almost frozen in disbelief at the brazen and incompetent manner of their targets. Miller knew that they now had enough to pull these two in. Time to take them down: he gave the order to move in.

The team rose up from their positions around the edge of the quarry and from vantage points along the tops of the precarious paths that ran down to the bottom. They started to edge towards the two men, still attacking the safe with hammer and crowbar and showing no signs of noticing the approaching police. The darkness covered this well.

And that was the problem: it was a black enough night when you were near the top of the quarry, but as you got towards the base, then it became like seeing through tar. Mellor and Beddoe scrambled down as best they could, trying not to be pulled by the dogs, who were surer-footed but were still on the leash, straining hard as they made for the foot of the incline.

There was a shout from Miller, and stabs of torch-beam light penetrated the black. The two men standing over the safe were suddenly aware that they were not alone. As the lights crossed and hit them, their surprise was obvious: but this sudden shock did not stop them from trying to make an escape. Leaving the safe, they ran in opposite directions.

Mellor was now on the floor of the quarry, and he let loose his dog. It sprang across the quarry floor, a blur of shadow as it sped towards one of the fleeing criminals. Mellor was on its tail as it took down its man. He was cuffed and under arrest before he knew what had hit him.

The other man rode his luck a little better: in the enveloping darkness, with the surveillance team hitting ground level at different places and in a staggered order, it was sometimes difficult to see who was who, let alone follow the progress of the man on the loose. Driven by fear and panic, he threaded between the scrub along the quarry floor and the approaching police.

Beddoe had been behind Mellor and could see that the man was headed for the rope they had skimmed down to reach the bottom. If he reached that, he could get himself out of reach of the men on the quarry floor and perhaps be up top before they could make their way back up. There should be someone still up there, but just in case…

Making a decision that would prove vital, he gave Major a command and the dog stopped, changing his direction. Beddoe had been his handler since he was a pup, and at four years he was in the prime of his working life. Lean, tightly muscled, and a smart animal, he was exactly what they would need if the perpetrator made the top of the quarry and had a clear run.

The drop into the quarry was a 120 feet. With an agility born of his panic and fear, the perpetrator was clambering up the rope at speed. Major and Beddoe were taking the side of the quarry that had a slope not a drop: you could climb it, but the incline made it more than a 120-foot path to the top. As they neared the top of that path, Beddoe let Major go with the command to stop his man. The dog raced off into the darkness as the criminal reached the lip of the quarry, hauled himself over and disappeared from view.

Beddoe reached the top of the quarry and looked around in the darkness. It was hard to see shapes against black mass of trees that formed the dense woodlands beyond the quarry. He scanned the area anxiously, but there was no sign of the criminal.

And no sign of the dog…

Chase

THERE WAS no witness to what happened next, and Major could not tell. However, from what was later discovered from Ian Augustus Jones after his subsequent arrest, and knowing how police dog training works, it's not too much of a stretch to imagine how the chase progressed.

The escaping man ran for the woodlands, knowing that he would be almost impossible to follow given the lead he had on the police team.

The darkness of the night, and the tightly packed trees through which he was now weaving were his allies. He collided with branches, stumbled over roots, and somehow managed to keep his footing, adrenaline pushing through his laboured breathing and aching limbs. Shinning up the rope and then running at full pelt was taking its toll. Yet he couldn't rest until he knew he was in the clear.

He wasn't yet: he could hear something crashing through the undergrowth behind him…

Major was on his trail. Reaching the top of the quarry and knowing that the man running ahead – the only man in sight – was the target his handler had commanded him to stop, the dog dived into the woodland and found his quarry's trail.

The physical trail was there: the broken branches and crushed vegetation that had been left by the quarry's flight would have sufficed in daylight, but Major had more than that. His training enabled him to pick up the air scent of the fleeing man and use this to follow his path. The scent would also be left along his ground track, reinforcing the strength of the trail the dog could follow.

His hearing told him that the man was ahead, and that he was breathing heavily. He could tell that he was gaining.

But where was his handler?

Search

MELLOR HAD his man in custody. Up the top of the quarry, the surveillance team gathered as Miller sifted confused eye-witness accounts as to what had happened to the other man. The confusion was inevitable in the dark night, but Beddoe was able to confirm that the man had reached the top and Major had been set after him. After that, the night had caused him to lose sight of them.

Miller asked, 'Did you try calling him back?' Beddoe must have looked at him as though it was a question beneath contempt. 'Of course I have, and he hasn't responded. That's not like him. What if something's happened and he's been injured? What if that's why he's not come back?'

Miller asked if it was possible that the man Major was chasing had doubled back and had tried to hide in the quarry, perhaps injuring the dog along the way? The Inspector couldn't see the woods being inviting for a clean getaway: come back, lay low, wait until morning and the police have left? It wouldn't be the first time... Beddoe was doubtful, but it wasn't an impossible scenario...

It was still dark when the surveillance team made a search of the quarry from top to bottom. They were ostensibly searching for their target, but in truth most of them were thinking about Major and hoping that they would find him. Beddoe joined the search, and when they found no sign of dog or man, he didn't know what to think. All he really knew was that he was concerned about what had happened to Major.

Miller told him they would come back when it was daybreak. Get their prisoner booked in, get a team to have another search. 'Might at least find some indication of what has happened,' he said.

Beddoe thought about the last time he had seen Major, as he crested the lip of the quarry. The dog had been headed for the woods. He doubted that he had doubled back. He was in there somewhere, and too far away to respond to calls.

Major was a good dog, an excellent police dog, but he was on his own out there, with no way back to his handler.

What the hell was he doing?

Pursuit

THE MAN emerged from the edge of the wood and onto a

river bank. He stood for a moment, breathing heavily, trying to listen to the night sounds around him. It was definitely there, something was in pursuit. He could hear it coming through the trees, but with no sound of speech and with a footfall that was too light for a blundering man like himself. He remembered seeing his mate getting pinned by a police dog as he reached the rope and took a look back.

Bloody thing must be after me now, he thought. Or there was more than bloody one of them…

He took a look across the river: it wasn't too wide, and he wasn't a bad swimmer. If he could get across it, then he could get away from the dog. He was sure he had read somewhere that dogs lost a scent in water, so if he could get over, he'd be safe. He looked at the water, running and gurgling in the dark. It would be cold, too. He might get caught in a current, he might go under… or he could just give in and let a dog try and take him. If the dog was on his own… No, he'd seen how those things were trained.

He took a breath, slipped down the bank and into the water. He could wade out a couple of feet, and then it dropped deep, sweeping him off his feet. Ready for this, he struck out for the far shore.

He was in the water when Major reached the riverbank. For a moment the dog must have lost the scent as he reached the water, looking up and down, taking a few paces each way, trying to pick up any scent that was there. But then his quarry was out of the water on the other side. The dog would have been able to hear him, even in the dark, perhaps even pick up an air scent. Even if he couldn't track the scent, Major knew that his quarry had gone in the water, and that he could hear someone on the other side: this had to be his man.

As the criminal moved off through the sparser woodlands

and back towards a built-up area, so Major plunged into the river and swam across. By the time he was out of the water, his quarry was out of sight: but there was a trail, and Major picked it up, setting off at a slower pace as he could not see or hear his man ahead, but taking his time to follow the trail, just as he had been trained. He would follow this until he found his prey, then he would just wait until his handler caught up with him…

The Agony Of Waiting

BEDDOE AND a BTP team under Miller returned to the quarry when it was daylight. Looking down at the quarry floor, with the safe still sitting there waiting to be removed, it seemed hard to imagine how difficult it had been to see anything in the dark. The outlines of scrub and rock were clearly delineated, with little place for anyone or anything to hide. Even the safe – the thing the criminals should have made sure was covered – could be plainly seen.

A search was made, but there was no sign of either their perpetrator or Major. They followed the direction that Beddoe believed the dog to have run and made a search of the woodland until they came to the river. There was a clear trail through, which ended at the bank. The ground was too hard for footprints or pawprints, but it was obvious that both dog and man had traversed the water. The question was simply this: where did they go once that they were out the other side?

The Dog On The Pavement

IT WAS a matter of routine for a police dog to be reported when it was absent for any reason. The South Wales police were alerted, and a call was put out for Major. In theory, a police dog shouldn't be hard to spot. In fact, it was going to be down to chance. In the meantime, PC Beddoe had to sit and wait, filing his report of the previous night's operation, and wondering if he would ever see his dog again. He knew that Major had got over the river – but what had happened after that?

Again, this is only supposition, but is based on the information that came from piecing together reports. The man Major was trailing had got back into town and was making for home, feeling sure that he had shaken off the dog. He headed back towards Grangetown, which is only a short distance from the Cardiff Docks. From the location of the robbery, the safe had been moved across Cardiff Bay and past University Hospital to Leckwith and the disused quarry. Grangetown was along the Penarth Road which led back up from the hospital and Leckwith. By road it was a four mile round trip from Cardiff Bay to Grangetown, but to walk directly was only a two mile route. These boys had not opted to go far from home either in their robbery or in their hiding place.

Major had dried out from the river as he trailed his man from sparser woodlands into a built-up residential area, and then along the Penarth Road. To do this he had not just taken a route down quiet side streets, he had padded along busy arterial roads where the smells from traffic could overwhelm most other scents. It was now daylight, and although the dog was tired and hungry after his exertion, his training and his innate sense of purpose kicked in. He could ignore hunger and exhaustion as long as he found the man he had been asked to find. Then he would wait.

Nothing much happened for the rest of the day. While Beddoe waited, trying to contain his concern, there were no sightings of Major or of the man they were seeking. It was only when it was reaching the evening that there was a development.

The local police station received a call from a young woman whose name was Annetta. She reported that a dog was sitting on the pavement in Penarth Road. It was an Alsatian, and it looked exhausted and bedraggled. It had been there all day, and she had tried to get it to move, but it refused to budge. She had taken it food and water, and it had eaten the food and had a drink. As most police dogs tend not to accept anything except from their handler (or their handler's immediate family) this was an indication of how much the dog's exertions had taken from him. Yet still he was staying put, waiting for Alan Beddoe.

The local station was sure that this was the missing BTP dog that had been reported. Everything about it fit, so they called the BTP Control Room and asked for someone from the Transport Police to attend, so as to confirm whether or not this was the missing Major.

The first officer to respond to this was Inspector Tony Kitts, who was in the process of clocking off duty when the call came in. Kitts had been at the quarry and would know Major. With Alan Beddoe now off duty, the quickest course of action would be for him to attend and see if this dog was Major.

Kitts knew it was Major straight away, and he knew when he couldn't get the dog to respond or move that there must be a good reason for this. There were kids hanging around who were obviously interested in the dog, and Kitts asked them a few questions. It had been several hours since Major had first gone missing around the quarry area, and he had travelled a distance by road of about five miles from Leckwith to Grange-town. How long had he been sitting here?

From the answers, Kitts gathered that Major had first been spotted in position about four hours before, and the local kids had made a fuss of him – which he had allowed – and had tried to tempt him to follow them down the road – which he had not. He had remained steadfast, taking the food and water when Annetta had put it down for him, but not moving from his position. Kitts noted that this was directly outside the front door of a house. It had a basement and a couple of storeys, and looked like it had been converted into flats.

Was it possible that Major had travelled the five miles because he had been on his man's trail the whole time? Kitts knew that these dogs were capable of tracking, but this would have been some feat. After trying to get the dog to move again, and finding that he would move for no-one – except perhaps his handler – Kitts decided to get Beddoe down to Penarth Road, as well as other BTP CID personnel. It looked like they may have found their man. Or Major had, to be more precise…

'Look, I reckon we've found your dog, and we might have found a whole lot more besides…'

When Beddoe and the other officers arrived, they were in the company of Vic Miller, who was hopeful that Major had stayed on the case and that he had succeeded in tracking the escaped man. If he had, given the number of scents that must have crossed that trail, it was an achievement that deserved their full attention.

Miller told his men that they would go in the front of the house as they had the necessary to effect entry. He detailed Beddoe to go around the back with Major. Their job would be to take the rear of the house, where the garden backed on to a ginnel, in order that anyone making a break could be taken before getting away. Another rapid escape for their man was not going to be on the cards. Not this time.

In the interval between being alerted and arriving on the scene, the BTP had liaised with their colleagues in the Cardiff Police and obtained information that the man they were seeking may possibly be hiding in the basement flat of the building. This was where the CID started. They effected entry and went through the rooms of the flat. They were empty. There were signs that it had been in use at least the day before, but no indication of whether or not someone had been there in the morning.

Was it possible that the dog had trailed his man back here, and that at some point he had left via the back, having seen the dog outside? Or was it possible that the dog had got it wrong? A look out the back gave no indication of any recent activity; the garden was overgrown, and it didn't look like anything had been trodden down, or any of the junk in there moved.

The CID men moved on to the other floors of the house, gaining entry to the other flats in the building. Those tenants had nothing to hide: there was no sign of their man anywhere. Frustrated, Miller checked in with the Cardiff Police. Their information was that the man they were looking for had been holed up in the basement flat. The source of the information was adamant.

And so was Major. The flat was searched for a second time, and the result was the same: nothing. Miller called Beddoe and Major around to the front of the building, as there was obviously no-one who was going to bother them at the rear. He briefed his men that their search had turned up nothing, so they would have to go back to base and work out another course of action. Some returned to their cars, ready to leave, while a few finished up inside. Beddoe had his van for the dog, but as he tried to get Major to get in the back, the dog resisted and pulled away. He returned to the front of the house, where he took up his position once more. When Beddoe tried to get him to move, he refused. PC Beddoe was a good handler, with good instincts, and he was sure that Major was telling them something. Despite all evidence to the contrary, Major was convinced that their man was still in the house.

Miller was exasperated at first when Beddoe called him over. 'Your man's still in there,' he told him. Miller insisted that the place had been thoroughly searched – twice – and that their man was not in there. But when Beddoe showed him how Major was intransigent – 'Look at him, he didn't stand out here for nothing, and he still won't bloody move' - and refused to respond to commands about which he usually no hesitation, Miller conceded that this was so out of character, and so insistent, that they had to take some action.

The one sure way of finding any suspect anywhere in the flat, regardless of the two searches already made, was to let Major finish the job he had started. Getting those men who were still in the house out into the street, he let the dog have what he had been waiting for: the chance to get into the flat, with no distraction, and finish the job he had started.

Beddoe let Major loose with the command to find. The dog started to work his way methodically through the few rooms of the flat, as he had been trained. When he came to the bedroom, he stopped dead in front of the wardrobe, and started to bark. Beddoe called him away, but he would not move. Neither would he shut up. Miller and Beddoe exchanged glances. The Inspector pointed out that the wardrobe had been searched twice now, and had been empty. How many times did the dog want him to open an empty wardrobe? 'As many times as it takes to satisfy him,' Beddoe replied, indicating the dog, who was still barking at the wardrobe.

Miller told Beddoe he should have a go at searching it, then. The PC opened the wardrobe and swept aside the few clothes hanging there. It looked empty enough, but he knew his dog well enough to trust him. There had to be something…

A slow grin crossed his face: considering the size of the wardrobe, it looked a bit shallow... He tapped at the back, and was answered by a hollow sound. A tap towards the middle, and it sounded surprisingly solid. A few more taps, and the false back to the wardrobe gave way, revealing their suspect, standing in the narrow enclosure. Arresting him, Beddoe turned to look at Major, who had stopped barking. It was only his fancy, he was sure, but he would swear for years after that he could almost see that dog grinning broadly.

The Dog Is Rarely Wrong

THE LESSON here is that if Major had been allowed to follow his instinct and if Beddoe had been allowed by the other officers to let the dog do his job from the moment they arrived, then they could have saved themselves a whole lot of time. As it was, two days later, the man in wardrobe pleaded guilty to several criminal offences connected to the robbery at Cardiff Magistrates Court, and was sentenced to six months in prison.

This conclusion could only be reached because Major pulled off an incredible tracking feat, through the quarry and adjacent woods, across the river and along busy arterial roads for a distance of five miles without any guidance or assistance from his handler. He could go no further having been confronted by a locked door. He simply sat down and waited patiently for his handler and for any other officers to arrive. His actions showed an incredible intelligence, persistence, and tenacity. He did what had been asked of him, despite the fact that it led him far from his handler and into a situation where he had no idea what he would face.

This remarkable story was one that Alan Beddoe was asked to recount for police dog handler reunions and for those websites run by dog handlers and retired police officers for years after. Major had a good career before retiring, but was never again faced with a situation that showed his cleverness and sense of duty in such a way. He had a happy retirement, and Alan Beddoe was still telling the story with a sense of amazement and pride in his dog until he, too, passed away in 2024.

This story is a testament not just to Major and Alan Beddoe, but also to how the training of police dogs concentrates on the aspects of a dog's capabilities and assets, and hones them until the dog becomes a highly skilled police operative.

Leaps and Bounds

WHILE THE BTP had been having issues that had stalled their development, other forces across the country had continued to develop and grow. The changing of boundaries and amalgamation of forces did not always help this to be steady and consistent, but nonetheless, the use of dogs became widespread in the years between Rex III and Major.

Down in Devon, by 1965 they had expanded their dog section to nine handlers and six dogs, which is an odd figure as it was usual to have at least as many dogs as handlers. But they did things their own way, and it worked: Feral and Astor had been used in tracking and apprehending escapees from HMP Dartmoor in this time, and were instrumental in convicting bank robbers who had committed their crime in Plymouth and abandoned their vehicle in Plymstock. A seeming dead end was turned into a result when the dogs tracked from the abandoned car to a road where the robbers picked up a second vehicle which was later identified. The evidence from the dog handler of the tracking established a link which enabled a conviction.

In Cornwall, they had proposed a formal dog section in 1959, but this proposal was put on hold until 1964, when the Cornwall Constabulary Dog Section was formed, with their first handler travelling to Staffordshire for training. Their informal use of dogs was seemingly considered ad hoc and reasonable enough to allow the local committees to avoid the use of the public purse until Chief Constable Kenneth Wherly lobbied hard enough. His efforts must have seemed in vain as Cornwall Constabulary ceased to exist in its own right in 1967, when it was merged with Devon and the separate force that operated in Plymouth. This did allow the combined force to grow to 15 handlers. One of the duties undertaken by these handlers was to patrol with the dogs at HMP Dartmoor, which they did for about a year until 1968 when newly trained prison dog handlers took over. (Prison dogs are a separate national section, not part of the police, and have a history of their own well worth recording.)

The dog section for the amalgamated force continued to grow in size and showed their handlers' skills in national dog trials, where they achieved exceptional results. The trials may seem showy to some, but they are an excellent way of judging the training levels and attainments of a dog section outside the area of deployment.

It was no wonder that Devon and Cornwall Constabulary had such good results and they would later become trailblazers in two distinct areas of dog training showing the forward thinking of the men in charge. The first is the Air Support Unit, which was formed in 1980, and looked at training and deployment of dogs in helicopters. This is now common for most dog sections, but had not been considered before the formation of this unit. Its origins came as a result of two things: the need to transport dogs quickly across the vast moorlands of the counties when the dogs were required for tracking escaped prisoners; and the deployment of dogs on freighters.

In the year of its inception, the Unit was called upon to search the vast cargo holds of the freighter 'Sealand Resource' off the coast at Brixham, in search of two stowaways. PD's Rex and King, with their handlers PC's Harris and Fitzgerald, proved the worth of the section by finding their targets rapidly. The same year, PD Sam and his handler PC Shorter apprehended three escapees from HMP Channings Wood in less than half an hour, earning a commendation in the process.

The section's second great innovation came over three decades later, in 2016, with the training of the country's first Digital Storage Detection Dogs. These are sniffer dogs that can detect USBs, hard drives, and other digital storage devices. This is highly specialised and is a vital tool in the digital age, working in the field of detection for money laundering, fraud, and child exploitation. In the first year this programme ran, the two dogs – Rob, a black Labrador, and Tweed, a Springer Spaniel – were loaned out for 50 assignments across the country. There are now dogs trained for this purpose in most forces as a result of training techniques evolved in Devon and Cornwall.

One of the forces that has taken this and run with it is Essex.

Thinking Out Of The Box...

WHAT IS Essex like? There's not really any other county like it: sandwiched between the rural idyll of Suffolk and the urban sprawl of London, Essex police find themselves encroaching on London territory and standing in the middle of farmland, possibly on the same day. Surrey – that most sensible and forward thinking of Constabularies from early days – lay to the south of London where urban lands slowly disappear and fade into woodlands. In the north east, it's another story. Turn the corner and you go from the Badlands of Basildon to fields of corn. It's harder, faster, different...

Essex seems to be a home for eccentric thinkers when it comes to dog sections. For some time, their dog recruitment was as haphazard as many forces but was fuelled by the instincts of a little old lady who ran a kennel. Vera was an Essex legend. Only in Essex would your dog recruitment be in the hands of a pensioner; and it was only in Essex that you would see an attempt to start training bloodhounds again over 60 years after they were last officially used by any force...

Originally, the dog unit had its headquarters in the main police building in Chelmsford, where the first two dogs Remoh, a Doberman, and Senta, a German Shepherd arrived in 1953. They had been purchased from Mount Browne in Surrey, and their handlers PCs Cousin and Hare were forced to share a van as the section was so new. Their first arrest came in 1955 when they tracked the robber of the Cherry Tree pub in Colchester across fields to an army camp, where they identified a serving soldier as the perpetrator.

This success led to an increase to 10 dogs and 10 handlers in 1956, and by 1968 they had been split across the county for greater coverage, stationed in Brentwood, Harlow, Colchester, and Thorpe. Laindon, near Basildon, was later added, and now they are at Rochford, South Ockendon and Bocking.

The main base of the dog unit was a purpose built facility at Sandon, outside Chelmsford, which has been purpose built in 1970. It was here that the first police bloodhound for nearly six decades arrived in 1998. That year, handler PC Malcolm Fish received a Home Office grant to train bloodhounds in following specific human scents, even in crowded and busy areas. The theory was that as human scent can still be detected for many days, so his dogs should be able to track one-day old scents in an urban area and over a week old in vegetated areas such as woodland and farmland. Bloodhounds are able to track even when it is no more than an air scent: so can most dogs, but not for as long after an event as a bloodhound. As we've seen before, bloodhounds were not the miracle workers this suggests, and Fish's theory was that this was due to their training, and not their natural capability. Simply put, they are more stubborn and harder to train than other dogs.

Two bloodhounds arrived as 14-week-old puppies – Sherlock and Morse, which is a very Essex sense of humour – and were allocated to handlers PCs Houlding and Smith. Their success was limited in practical results, but proved Fish's point to a degree. Bloodhounds are still not commonly used, but Fish's progress showed that out of the box thinking can get results, and Essex still keep two bloodhounds on a roster that includes 42 German Shepherds and 10 recovery dogs of varying breeds.

Low-key Midlands and Hampshire Developments

IN CONTRAST to most of the forces mentioned so far, in the West Midlands they went about their business with no fuss, but with a steady development that showed careful planning and an eye on steady growth. They have no history of early misfires and no out of box thinking; there is no real record of any unorthodox adoption of dogs as there was in the West Country, and no uptake of dogs and then a sudden dropping until a sudden rethink, as in Glasgow.

The first police dog in the Midlands region was bought by the Walsall Borough Police in August 1939, after a talk on police dogs had impressed the local Watch Committee enough for them to devote some budget to recruitment and training. They sent PC George Cleobury off on training with a black Labrador called Don.

That date is worth noting: one month before World War Two was declared. As those forces that had experimented with dogs were dropping them, the Midlands was taking up the challenge. The declaration of war was not a surprise, and most Councils and Watch Committees were preparing for a war footing. Budget and manpower were to be deployed on lines that did not include dogs.

Whatever prompted the Committee's decision to press on, it meant that post-war they were well prepared to build their dog sections across the cities of the Midlands, with Birmingham gaining its first dog in 1951: an Alsatian named Flash, handled by PC John Blackhall.

When Coventry appointed the first three dog handlers to its local force in 1961, they had three dogs named Flame, Blaze and Dante, who were named by Chief Constable Edward Pendleton as a tribute to the people lost in the Blitz that decimated Coventry during the war. Pendleton had been a serving officer in the city during this time, and chose the names to reflect the fires that had raged from the bombing.

In a similar manner to the West Midlands, the Hampshire Constabulary were also developing a dog section with little fuss. Unlike their West Midlands counterparts – but like so many Constabularies post-war – they had been reliant on the Surrey expertise at Mount Browne to aid them.

Hampshire's use of dogs began with the recruitment of Mountbrowne Quaker in 1952, along with Mountbrowne Wendy, two dogs raised and trained in the Mount Browne breeding programme. They were handled by PCs Jack Ryles and Ron French respectively. After assisting the force that looked after the New Forest, Hampshire in conjunction with the Isle Of Wight force also purchased Mountbrowne Orris. Thus the first three dogs in Hampshire all came from the kennel at Mount Browne and were part of their breeding programme. By 1957 Portsmouth had their own dog section, and their most notable dog in the early years was handled by PC John Tolcher: the dog served nine and a half years before his age caught up with him, which is a remarkably long stint as a police dog. Usually, they are retired after about seven years average service. This splendid animal was Mountbrowne Ingot, another of the Surrey breeding programme dogs. The first Hampshire drug detection dog was Roddy, out of Southampton, trained and in deployment from 1972.

The Hampshire dog section, which also covers the Isle Of Wight, grew to a strength of 31 dogs and an equal number of handlers. This growth and development can once more be traced back to the work done by the Surrey Constabulary at their Mount Browne centre.

Hampshire, by their own admission, leaned heavily on Surrey during their early years. There is no shame in this: the desire to develop requires you to look to the best, and at that time, Surrey was the hothouse of police dog innovation.

Certainly, you could make a case for their work in the second half of the 20th century being the driving force that leads us to today.

Dog handler Elaine Michaels pictured with Taz the German Shepherd.
Zippy the Fox Terrier hard at work (top picture, right-hand page)

PART FOUR 🐾🐾🐾🐾
The New Millennium

New Era, New Advances

CSI: Canine Superior Instinct

THE ADVANCES in technology since the turn of a new century have been immense. Some aspects of old school policing and investigation may seem archaic and obsolete. But there is always room for the wisdom and accumulated knowledge of the past to work with the new, to create a more efficient form of policing. This is as true of the police dog as in any other area of policing: to tap into the growing knowledge of just what a dog is capable of, and meld that to new advances in forensic science, have given us a whole new breed of trained animal.

New Skills, Greater Successes: DNA Dogs

MAJOR WAS a general-purpose dog, and he showed how even those who are not specialist sniffer dogs can perform incredible feats of tracking. There are also those dogs whose skills are so specialised and niche that their successes are rarely known. These are the dogs that specialise in DNA and cadaver search.

These dogs come under the category of Forensic Search Dogs and have highly specialised training in locating blood or semen. They have an advantage for use when the scene of a crime has no clearly defined areas where there may be DNA-based evidence to gather as they can provide a quick elimination of 'clean' areas, enabling those with more conventional and recognised techniques to focus their search.

Even then, when the area requiring analysis is defined, the nose of the highly trained dog has a distinct advantage. As the use of the chemical Luminol is the only effective way for the crime scene investigation team to test for blood, they can be hampered by conditions. In order to detect blood, the chemical reacts with haemoglobin to cause a reaction known as chemi-luminescence. This gives off a glow when ultraviolet light is shone on it. The problem being that in order to get the conditions for this to work, an area has to be completely blacked out.

So, you have to find the right area, black it out, spray thoroughly, and make sure that anything you find is in your direct line of sight, or else it can be missed. This takes time and is expensive: two types of cost that are a problem in modern policing. Not to mention it can only be used indoors as outside is almost impossible to black out; or that you can get a false positive if someone happens to have sprayed something like household bleach around, making kitchens and bathrooms an issue; or that luminol has the possibility of eradicating other evidence when used.

You don't have any of those problems with a dog: it just needs its nose and to know what scent it is looking for. It can find an area in darkness and light, and as it is looking purely for the scent it has been trained to find, it can eliminate the kind of false positives obtained by luminol. The dog searches three-dimensionally and can indicate an area anywhere in a building quickly, without painstaking and time-consuming spraying. Humans tend to search two dimensionally, relying only on their line of sight.

Dogs really are remarkable creatures, having approximately 200 million olfactory receptors in their noses, which means an ability to find and distinguish a scent which is 40 times greater than the average human nose.

The detection of semen also presents the crime scene investigator with the same kind of issues that they face with blood. The search for semen evidence is by the use of black light. Because the element phosphorus is present in semen, any trace will show up by glowing under black light. If you think of white clothing glowing under lights in a disco, you'll have some idea of what this looks like. The problem is that other substances that may contain such elements also give off a glow under black light: highlighter pen is a perfect example of this.

Given these issues, a Forensic Search Dog is an excellent search tool. They can be trained to work on land or water; their ability to home in on one scent makes them incredibly efficient in time and expenditure; they cannot spoil evidence with DNA contamination, as can sometimes happen in crime scenes with investigators, as canine DNA does not react with human DNA; they can work in the kinds of enclosed spaces such as vehicles that present problems for crime scene investigators using cumbersome equipment and needing eyeline.

The key use of semen detection has been described as making all the difference in a rape or sexual assault investigation, in particular when the suspect denies any such activity taking place. DNA detected by a dog can prove in the first instance that they are lying about events, and from there it provides a bedrock on which an investigation and a case can be built. This was shown starkly in an investigation in Nottingham in 2021, where a man was being investigated over allegations of sexual offences committed against teenage girls several years before. A key piece of evidence gathered against him was a semen deposit recovered from a bedroom which helped to prove the veracity of an account that had been given by one victim. The case built from this foundation led to a conviction and a sentence of 24 years for the perpetrator.

Speaking to dog handlers during the course of this book, two other instances in recent years came to light. In each instance, the ability of the dog led to a conclusion to the investigations, both helping to prove guilt and also to confirm innocence. This is the benefit of such a dog: they can eliminate the doubt on either side of the divide. Because of the sensitivity of these cases, they can only really be talked about in non-specific terms. Some details have been removed or changed to protect the identity of those involved.

The first concerns a young girl whose relative was under suspicion for sexually assaulting her. There was no physical evidence to back up the claims until a dog was called in: the girl had spoken of her relative perpetrating one of the assaults in a clearing near his home. The open nature of the location – a clearing in a wood, with grass, moss and wild flowers – meant that it was almost impossible for a crime scene investigation team to search for physical evidence. Everything that hampers such a search – no specific area in a large clearing, no easy way to blackout any search area selected, the possibility of contamination, finding a two-dimensional eyeline to search – was present. It was only the trained nose of a Forensic Search Dog, searching for a specific scent, that could stand any chance of securing the evidence. A single drop of semen on a leaf found by the dog yielded the DNA evidence to tie the girl's relative to the site, and confirm her story. From there, the case built led to his conviction.

Conversely, a male carer in a nursing home found himself under suspicion when he was accused by an elderly female resident of sexually assaulting her. It was his word against hers. She did not have dementia, though there was a question mark raised over her diminishing capability as she was vague about where the assault took place, and some details surrounding it. Mud sticks, and even if her claims could not be proven, there would always be a question mark that would follow the male carer both at that job, and at any subsequent post he applied for.

The matter could be settled by a Forensic Search Dog, who could go into all the areas that the carer and his accuser had been together and effect a wide-ranging search. The dog was also given all of the woman's clothes to search through. When, after all areas and all of the clothing had yielded no result, and the dog had found nothing, it helped in establishing the carer's innocence, as even the slightest scent of DNA from semen would have got the dog to respond.

A conviction where the perpetrator could easily have escaped prosecution, and no charges being brought when the complete lack of evidence could prove the truth of the accused's statement: the scales of justice balanced by the nose of a highly-skilled canine.

The Dogs Of Death

THERE IS ONE other function for Forensic Search Dogs that has a vital role to play in police work, but is one that is little known to the public as it involves the kind of search that many of us would perhaps rather not think about: the search for the deceased, who may have been missing and dead for some time.

These dogs can play a key role in resolving missing persons cases and unresolved murders, providing not just vital evidence to the forces of the law, but closure to families that will then allow them to grieve properly.

The search for cadavers – corpses or sometimes just the remains of those deceased for a long time – is something that the dog is well suited to because of its large number of olfactory receptors. The average is around 200 million: this does vary according to breed, and many cadaver dogs are German Shepherds as they average 225 million, whereas a Dachshund may have a much lower total, say around 125 million. This gives the German Shepherd a much greater advantage in being able to refine the scent it searches for, and to detect a much fainter trace. However, all dogs have the ability to detect a cadaver: it's just that some can detect those buried deeper, or who have been in the ground longer – anything that may cause a deterioration in the strength of the scent.

The difference between a cadaver dog and a general search and rescue dog is that while the latter are trained for the general scent of a human, the former has specialist training that concentrates on the detection of that particular scent which is given off by decomposing human flesh: a particular combination of chemicals that is released when decomposition takes place. For this reason, in many missing persons searches both types of dog are used, so that there is a greater chance of recovering the missing person, alive or dead.

The dogs are trained for trailing, so that they can pick up the scent of a dead body that may have been dragged across the ground; and for air scenting, so that they may pick up any scent of decomposition that remains in the air, and so follow this to the source and recover the remains. They have an incredible success rate of 95%, and have been known to detect remains buried up to 15 feet – approximately five metres – underground.

But how can they be trained ? Are they trained with the use of human remains? Not initially: there are certified training facilities where chemicals are blended in a particular combination to mimic the scent of decomposing flesh. When the dog has proven itself on these, then it is moved on to train with actual body parts. These are provided by those who will donate their bodies for scientific research and experiment, and who have donated themselves for forensic training amongst other disciplines. It is only after the dog has then proven its efficiency over an average period of more than 1,000 hours of training that it is allowed to work in the field.

A common question people have about these dogs is how, in somewhere like woodlands, can a dog discriminate between the scent of decomposing human remains and the remains of any wildlife that may be in the area. The answer lies in the fact that human and animal decomposition have very different chemical compositions, and one of the refinements in developing cadaver training was to teach the dog to recognise the difference and concentrate only on the human scent.

Of course, this means that training a cadaver dog is expensive. At a time when police forces in the UK are looking to ever tighter budgets and have their eye on the dog sections, this could be queried. While the general purpose dog or sniffer that is not so specialised may raise questions about cost in the field (no matter how unjustified these may be), the efficacy of a Forensic Search Dog, particularly a cadaver dog cannot be questioned. They may cost more in terms of training and continued maintenance, but the hours they can save in crime scene investigation when the circumstances dictate, and the money they can save in wasted site tests by being able to home in and refine a search, cannot be denied.

In fact, the use of dogs to detect dead bodies is nothing new: it's been proven by research that they were being used as far back as 700BC to track the dead, and there have been countless reports over the centuries of dogs who have shown an amazing ability to sniff out decomposing flesh and remains, whether they be a few hours old, or lain buried for decades.

The advance in recent years comes from the refinement of training to ensure that the dog has a better understanding of the scent it is dispatched to track. This they can do even if a body has been removed from one scene to another. There are instances when a dog has identified a crime scene, and then been able to track and identify where the body in question has been taken.

This kind of work may seem a long way from Major tracking his man from a quarry to a wardrobe, and Rex III learning how to become a sniffer dog for drugs, but in truth they are very much a part of the same thing.

Above all, it is the bond between human and dog that makes this possible. The dog's intelligence in learning this skill combined with the human's understanding of the dog is what enables the police to work so well with canines. Something that is vital in the new era, but also something that can sometimes have unexpected and traumatic results.

Taz: The Cost Of Duty

Turning Point

JUNE 2011. It's dark. The night has been made all the more oppressive by the silence that has fallen over the house in a quiet road in Braintree, Essex. Inside the house there is a family being held hostage by the mother's abusive ex-partner. A stealth team keeps surveillance outside, looking for any signs of movement and to keep any indication of police presence to a minimum.

An armed response team is waiting, as it is known that the abusive partner is also armed. They are waiting for a dog handler to arrive so the animal can go in ahead and scout out the ground for them. When they see that the handler on rota has arrived with Taz, they feel satisfied. A large, sleek and intelligent police dog with eyes that shine in the dark night, he is known to them and is a dog whose bravery and intelligence they trust. They know they can rely on him.

Taz proves reliable. Up to a point. Then something happens that does not endanger the armed response team, nor does it endanger hostages, as it proved to be far too late for that. What happens changes the lives of both dog and handler. It's an event that demonstrates that a police dog is more than just a four-legged machine. It's an event that demonstrates how the bond between dog and handler can be so strong that it can affect the way the dog views a situation. It shows an instance of incredible intelligence and empathy.

Taz's story is an important one as it can change the way we look at police dogs: we can see them as living, breathing and feeling creatures, as vulnerable to the stresses and unexpected shocks of the job as any police officer.

Heroism comes in many forms.

When we think of police dogs and bravery, we tend to think of those courageous animals that are injured in the line of action, receive medals, and are feted in the press. Whilst they deserve everything they get, there are many others who are equally courageous and have their careers cut short by events that are completely beyond their control.

Many have injuries sustained in the line of duty while others have congenital defects that suddenly appear and cause injury or disability that can get in the way of their work. For some dogs, traumatic events can have the same effect on an animal as it does on a human being. This may seem odd to hear, but the truth is that an animal is a being with intelligence and emotion that may not work in the same manner as that of a human being but can nonetheless be affected by events in a similar manner. Such was the case of Taz.

Taz was a superb police dog. One of the best of his generation. More than just a prime example of how the job is more than just being a protector or a sniffer dog. Taz was everything a police dog should be, and he worked in perfect harmony with his handler.

The problem, of course, is that this may have been his downfall. His bravery and career were cut short by a traumatic event. It's easy to forget that dogs are sentient beings that have emotional responses. They have a certain sensitivity and this is what enables them to fulfil their training and work effectively. The issue is that they may not show these things in the same way as humans, and so it becomes hard to spot. Not, perhaps, for the handler who really knows their dog. Generally, though, things may seem normal. Nonetheless, the effect is still there, hidden behind their eyes.

Taz came to Essex Police by way of donation. Many dogs were recruited this way, and it could sometimes cause issues. If you breed a police dog from a line of dogs in service, then you have a better chance of knowing what you are likely to get. However, it was common practice for most Forces to acquire at least some of their dogs from kennels that were trusted, and which took in waifs and strays. Some excellent dogs came this way, Taz being one of them. But he was an exception in that he had no issues or quirks: other dogs may have seemed to be a good fit on the surface, but incidents in their past had left traces in their behaviour which could cause future issues.

The Perfect Occupation

TAZ WAS handled by Elaine Michaels. From the age of 13, Elaine had wanted to join the police. She still has the school-book in which she cut out pictures of police dogs and handlers and wrote in great detail about how she would like to join the police and become a dog handler. There was only one problem with this: at the time she was writing, there were no female handlers in her local force – Essex – and so she was certain that this was not a realistic option. The first female handler in Essex was Lesley Rosenwald, who was appointed some years after Elaine's schooldays.

Still an exclusively male field when Elaine finished school, she did not join the force immediately upon graduating and she took up a number of other jobs instead. When she eventually did join the police force in 1994, it was out of a sense of frustration following a crime in which she was the victim.

At this time, Elaine was living in Halstead and was known as a petrol-head. Cars had always been a passion of hers, and she belonged to a car club for customised vehicles. She was obsessed with engines and customising cars. She had an old Ford Escort that she had done a lot of work on, and of which she was very proud. Unfortunately, the downside of it being an old car was that it was easy to break into: far too easy.

'When it was stolen, I reported the theft,' Elaine recalled, 'and then nothing happened for a long time, until I got a call out of the blue to say that the car had turned up in a field in Bedford, burnt out. When I went to the local station to find out how to get it back, they told me that it was none of their business and that as I was the owner, I would have to arrange my own pick-up.'

She was not impressed. Annoyed at being told she would have to tow away her own burnt out – not to mention stolen – vehicle, she decided that she needed to do something about it. Driven by her own anger and determined that she could do a better job, she joined the Essex police force as a Special Constable and, after a while in the job, worked her way up to Section Officer. This period also re-ignited her childhood desire of being a dog handler. After applying to be a full-time police officer, it took another nine years to get into the dog section.

Elaine had been warned it would be hard: 'It was known as "dead man's shoes" as there were only a limited number of handlers, and no-one likes to relinquish the job. It took hard graft and evidence of being able to work alone and be pro-active – and having the patience to wait for a vacancy.'

Even then, there were still obstacles. Although the women's section of the force had been integrated in 1975, there were still enough older officers who remembered the days before, and with some resentment for the change.

First came the written application, then a week-long suitability course. The course itself was residential, at Sandon, Essex Police's training centre. A local charity kennel supplied the dogs, random breeds, and the idea was that the potential handler should show an ability to bond with the dog and improve its behaviour.

This was where she knew she would have to work harder than the rest to prove herself. 'The dogs were chosen by the trainers, and I was handed a Shepherd bitch that no-one could get out of its kennel,' she said. 'It was the only Shepherd, was aggressive and had issues, and they said they were giving it to me as "it only liked women". The kennel hands could not persuade it out of its kennel, and I had to entice the dog out. After successfully getting her out, I was then called back at weekends to walk the dog after the course had finished and before it went back to the charity kennels.'

Having passed this, the interview process came next. Elaine was accepted but still found herself the last out of five handlers from the suitability course to be posted to the dog section. This took two years of waiting, and the clock was ticking as there is a two-year cut-off point after which successful applications are no longer valid, and the potential handler has to start again. When she went to see the dog section Sergeant, he told her that there was a rumour going around that as soon as she was in the section, she would apply to be part-time. She had no idea where this rumour had come from, and she immediately put him right. His response was that as soon as any handler puts their head above the parapet, someone wants to chop it off…

Shortly after this encounter, she got a posting. She had finally achieved her dream, it seemed. The work was hard, being a single mum and trying to juggle the childcare of three small children with working as a dog handler. A dog section is small, and Essex is a large county to cover, so the work was demanding in terms of distance travelled as much as duty. At this time there were five dogs on shift at any given time. The dog section worked on a rota and shift system to cover days and nights, and Elaine was covering North Essex, based out of Colchester.

False Starts...

THE FIRST dog Elaine was allocated was called Hooch. She said: 'He was a furry, long-coated German Shepherd with a reddish colouring and a pointed snout that made him look almost fox-like. He was a good dog, he trained well. The only problem was he lacked aggression.'

An unfortunate shortcoming as this is a necessary trait for a police dog. Elaine realised this would be an issue when she was on crowd control in Colchester, in full riot gear and facing a crowd of protestors. Hooch was at her side. He was supposed to look threatening; he was supposed to be a dog that looked like he meant business. In actual fact, he stood facing the crowds with his tail wagging and a stupid grin on his face. He was excited, but not in the way he was supposed to be.

In truth, he looked like he wanted to play. This was not the impression he was supposed to create, and it didn't escape the notice of some of the protestors, who found it hilarious. As if this wasn't bad enough, after they stood down, the officer who had been beside her on the front line remarked with heavy sarcasm, 'He looks more like he wants to go and join that lot, not keep them at arm's length.'

Despite his gorgeous looks and the fact that he was in many ways a good dog at other aspects of the job, Hooch had to go.

Elaine's next dog was called Arnie. That was not his original name, but she renamed him after Arnold Schwarzenneger, possibly in the hope that it would toughen him up. He was another German Shepherd because, at this time, Elaine was working with general purpose dogs rather than single purpose, and the Shepherd was generally the default breed of choice.

Arnie was a good dog in training, but he had one major problem: He hated traffic.

'He had this terrible fear of passing cars,' Elaine explained. She knew this would be a problem, and that he might not be much good out on the streets. One cold night she was called out to Military Road in Colchester – a very busy thoroughfare with a lot of traffic at any time of day or night.

The call-out had come from a paramedic who had picked up a patient and was having trouble with the woman's partner. A victim of domestic abuse, the woman was in the back of the ambulance and her partner had climbed in with her to continue the row and to assault her further. He refused to leave when asked and the paramedic was left with no option but to call the police.

Elaine arrived, got Arnie out of the back of the van, and went round to the back of the ambulance, where she asked the assailant to get out. He refused. There was not enough room for her to get into the back with the dog and force the removal of the assailant. The only thing she could do was to wind him up to such a pitch where he would come after her. Once in the open, he could be restrained, especially as she had the dog to assist her...

'I was revving up Arnie as I kept talking to him, ready to let him go when I'd got him out in the open. The main thing was to get him out of the confined space and into an area where I could tackle him, with the dog beside me.'

It looked like this was working: angered, he came out of the back of the ambulance, headed straight for her. She released

Arnie to move in and restrain the man. Unfortunately, this was not happening at some isolated spot. It was at the side of a busy road, with traffic roaring by despite the late hour. Off leash, Arnie took one look at the traffic and was stricken with terror. He did a U-turn and disappeared into the night. Elaine couldn't look back to see where the dog had gone as she now had a man twice her size headed for her, hell-bent on doing her harm. In her words, she took 'a bit of a battering', although she did manage to bear hug and restrain him before reinforcements arrived. It was only after he had been carted away that she was able to draw breath and wonder what had happened to the dog.

After the incident, one of the paramedics came up to her. 'Excuse me, do you want to know where your dog went?' When she nodded, he said, 'He ran back to the van and jumped in the back. He looked so scared that I shut the door to keep him there.'

And this was where she found him...

Obviously, this was not going to end well for Arnie. Elaine took him for a training scenario in the woods to try and test his mettle. But he failed this as well. A trail through the woods was prepared and Arnie completed the chase, but when faced with a perpetrator that he had to take down, he did not bite him. The trainer had a padded sleeve for such a purpose, as dogs are trained to take down a target in this manner, but Arnie ran away, unsure of what to do. Sadly, this confirmed he was not fit for purpose and would have left Elaine in yet more trouble.

As the dogs in Essex were being recruited from kennels, they were often turned in by people unable to cope with them or rescued. When you don't have a breeding programme that is specifically designed for police usage, you are going to have continuous problems. Essex lagged behind in this respect, as many other forces had started their own breeding programme by now. Surrey had been breeding their dogs since the 1960s.

Elaine believes this may have been the problem with both Hooch and Arnie. 'Any dog that's handed in has some issues,' she said. 'The problem is that these issues often don't come out until training is over and you're in the middle of a real situation. But then it's too late. And there's no way of knowing this until you are actually in the moment.'

Elaine was not the only handler to have behavioural difficulties with kennel dogs. After several incidents, a rethink in the force was inevitable and now, Essex breeds its dogs from pups like most other forces.

Back in the early 2000s, Elaine was still left with a problem. She needed a new dog. It would come in the usual way, through the kennels, but little did she know that she was about to find the dog of her dreams.

The Right Stuff

TAZ HAD been given in for police training by a couple who had originally used him for Schutzhund training. This is a sport that originated in Germany, as the name suggests: it means Protection Training and in it the dog is trained in tracking, obedience, and protection. It has a great similarity to the kind of training undertaken by a police dog and so, in this sense, Taz had already started on the road to being a working dog. His owners had suffered an illness that meant they could no longer compete, but they wanted Taz to be given the chance to continue as he loved the work. From Elaine's point of view, this was great as Taz had already shown himself to be good potential material. The downside meant that now she had a third dog and she had to undergo training yet again.

With general purpose dogs, like sniffer dogs, training is very much toy and reward-based these days. It's about the dog obeying the command to get the reward. Dogs are trained to track people by following ground scent and air scent. To track objects and to retrieve objects. They are trained in how to contain and also bring down a perpetrator that they are chasing. There are certain body parts that the dog is taught to grapple with in order to do this. Training also involves crowd and riot control, as a general purpose dog can be deployed in all of these scenarios.

The focus is on teamwork. 'The dog and handler train as a pair and are licenced as a pair,' Elaine explains. 'They are tied together. If a dog retires or a handler moves on, then there must be retraining for both.

'For instance, if a dog is retired on medical grounds or those of age, then the handler cannot just be given another dog. The handler must go through the training programme again, matched with the new dog. In the same way, if a handler finds that he cannot work with a dog and wants to hand him over to someone else, then that handler must undergo training with the dog from the very beginning.

'They are then licensed once more as a pair. Re-licensing for a handler and dog takes place once a year for general purpose dogs. A handler cannot go out to work on even one shift with a different dog, and a dog cannot be handed temporarily over to another handler unless they have a license which covers both of them.'

The importance of this lies in the close bond of communication that exists between dog and handler. The handler has to know that they can trust that dog implicitly to obey their every order, and know when the dog has to do something that the handler cannot necessarily give an order for. In the same way, the dog must have absolute faith in its handler that every order given will be correct and obeyed. The dog must know its handler well enough to be able to interpret their meaning when it cannot be made clear. This involves the reading of gesture and body language as much as what the dog can hear and see clearly. It also involves reading the mood of the handler.

It is this close bond that makes for a great dog/handler team, the kind Taz and Elaine were about to become. The very nebulous nature of this bond makes people sceptical about its existence, as it seems to be something for which there is no proof. However, almost a century and a half ago the psychologist and writer Maurice Maeterlinck observed that a horse which would apparently count numbers shown to it by its trainer was in fact reading subtle body language signals made by that trainer. The power of observation and understanding in animals that work closely with people – the ability of sheepdogs being a prime example – should not be underestimated.

Taz came along in 2004, and from the very beginning Elaine knew he was something different.

'He was another German Shepherd and was a large, powerful dog,' she recalled. 'Sleek and shiny with an intelligent look in his eye. There was just something about him that meant we formed a bond very quickly. Rarely do you get a dog who can bond with a handler like Taz did. He was special.'

The obvious question is why it took until her third dog for this to happen? The truth is that Elaine was far from alone in her struggles. It's partly the nature of having to train with dogs that have not been bred for the task, and partly a matter of luck of the draw. To get that sympatico relationship between handler and dog is not simply a matter of training.

But rarely did it come along like this. It's obvious looking at photographs of the pair of them, particularly when undertaking trials, that there was a strong connection. There is one photograph taken during a trial where Taz is in full flight beside Elaine and he is looking up at her for a cue. His face is a picture of absolute obedience and absolute devotion.

To talk about trials is possibly the quickest and simplest way to demonstrate their understanding, and also to outline the kind of skill that is required from a top-drawer animal. Trials are something that many handlers and dogs will do. They are organised on a national and regional basis. In them, the dogs undertake a number of exercises with their handlers in order to test their obedience, efficiency, speed and the manner in which they can complete a task. To achieve a high rating in these trials demands a high degree not just of skill and obedience, but of understanding between dog and handler.

Taz and Elaine came fifth in their trials. His particular skill was in tracking and searching. 'In tracking,' Elaine explained, 'the dogs work in straight lines, which are laid out in such a way that you have straight and diagonal lines that cross and connect, with some that come to a sudden end called "dead legs". The point of these ends are to emulate the sudden halt a dog would find when coming up against a wall or a river. Can the animal backtrack and pick up a fresh trail? As well as the scent trail, there are also objects placed along the trail, some of which are very small and partially buried. The dog's task is to scent and track these objects, then retrieve and mark them. In the past it was the dog's task to retrieve these objects and carry them back to the handler in their mouth. The practice now in retrieval is for the dog to find the object and then lay down, putting the object between its paws and wait for the handler to come over.'

This change in practice was led by the increase in forensic technology: whereas once the object being carried in a dog's mouth would make no difference, now it could very easily contaminate any evidence on the object it carried.

Using a dog in this way is a very good practical tool for the police and saves on both manpower and time.

'Suppose someone is stopped by a police officer after a chase, carrying tools for burglary,' Elaine explained. 'This is an offence known as "going equipped" under the Theft Act of 1968. It doesn't matter if a burglary has been committed or not at this point: there has still been a crime. When caught by the officer, the perpetrator flings his tools over a wall where they may land on a railway embankment, a building site, or wasteland that is overgrown. To search for it by hand would take a lot of manpower and time, combing the area carefully. One dog, however, can use its search skills to locate the objects and then stay, with the tools (in this instance) between its paws, secured and marked, until its handler arrives at the scene.'

These kinds of tasks would prove simple for Taz. He proved himself many times over as a tracker, and one of his finest exploits in this field was not an explosive event or even the press-worthy, but it meant he was able to save the life of a vulnerable person and do so while showing an incredible instinct and empathy for the situation.

The Working Dog

A PATIENT WAS missing from a mental health facility near Colchester. She was dangerous to herself and capable of self-harm. It was imperative that she be found as soon as possible. To this end, the dog section had been called in to track her as it would appear that she had wandered into the woods that were nearby to the facility. The use of dogs to track the missing and vulnerable is something that does not receive much attention, but it can be one of the most rewarding and important parts of the job. The elderly, the ill, those with mental health issues

– all of these need careful handling, and this is where a good handler and dog come into their own.

'Taz was able to trace her path through the woods by her scent,' Elaine recalls, 'even when it should have been difficult for him: the reason being that the woman had found a clearing and was sitting in the middle of it, having covered herself in petrol. She sat there holding a lighter. The smell of the petrol was overpowering and is something that all good tracker dogs find can obscure a scent. But Taz was able to keep enough of a trail going so that he could still locate her.'

Taz was leading the way, with Elaine behind, along with a team that could talk to the woman and try to defuse the situation she was in. She needed to be talked down, so that she did not harm herself. Usually when a suspect is located, the dog will indicate where they are by barking. However, with training, dogs will also know whether or not they should bark. They are able to judge when they can make a noise and when they need to withdraw and leave.

When Taz had located the woman he held back until he was sure that his handler and the specialist team were in sight. Only then did he withdraw at a non-verbal signal from Elaine. Most well-trained dogs are good at knowing which situations they should bark in, and which not. But Taz was just that little bit smarter, that little bit more empathic. True, it's a part of the training, but it's also a part of the training at which only some dogs can really excel. Taz was one of those.

Taz was a grounded dog: this is the term Elaine uses. When I asked her to explain the difference between Taz and some other police dogs, she said, 'The old way of training was designed to have hard dogs who were trained just for attack. It was all about having a dog that could be easily "revved up", which I always use to mean the dog would be primed to be let go at a perpetrator or assailant, a protection dog who would be able to handle himself in a violent or aggressive situation and respond to his handler in a way that was based on attack as a form of defence.'

For a general purpose dog, this made sense in the days when dogs were deployed mostly in the hunt for offenders, as a tracker and a tool for arrest, or else used for crowd control where they may face hostility that would require them to defend officers and themselves. While this made sense in the context of the time, the flipside was it made them unable to adapt and be used in different ways and different scenarios.

Elaine continued, 'With the old way, Taz's sensitivity with that mental health patient would not have been possible. An older, harder trained dog would probably have barked and caused that vulnerable person to act in a manner that could have been detrimental to her. The scenarios in which dogs are now deployed need a different type of training, and for a dog to have different responses both to the public, and to the handler.'

As she explained this, something came back to me from my days at primary school: I had a friend whose father was a handler, and they had a German Shepherd, then called an Alsatian. When there was a birthday party, or you were invited to tea, the dog was locked up in an upstairs bedroom or in a shed out in the back garden. I can remember going to the bathroom, or playing in the back garden, and hearing the dog bark furiously when I was nearby. I had a Golden Retriever at home, and I always supposed that he could smell my dog intruding on his space.

This dog would have been trained as a hard dog, as it was around 50 years ago, and although it may have been okay with the immediate family as it knew who they were and its training meant that it was hot-wired to keep them safe, it was more than hostile to any intruder when its handler was not close by.

Although things are changing, there was still, at the time Taz was working during the 2000s, a culture in the police that saw the dogs as tools rather than living and sentient beings. They could be collateral damage like any other piece of equipment, and the fact that they, too, may be affected by their work in some way, was an alien concept. That had to change. Not only because the experience of Taz and dogs like him demonstrates the fallacy of this concept, but because dogs are much more than just a piece of equipment. To use them at their best, it is necessary to train them in a different way, and to treat them as intelligent animals, not tools. The wide range of scenarios in which they can find themselves demands that of them and of their handlers. In order to do this, they need to be able to adjust to people and be sensitive to atmosphere and subtle changes in behaviour. They need to use their native intelligence in a way that the old, harder methods of training could never allow.

In essence, they do not need to be hyped up and kept in a constant state of tension and readiness for battle. They need to be sensitive to where they are. Grounded. This description fit Taz perfectly. Perhaps his early service training, geared to adapt to the demands of a potentially disabled owner when placed, and the sensitivity this requires, had brought out something in him that other dogs may have still buried; perhaps he did not have the early incidents that may have affected Hooch and Arnie and made them unsuitable for the work. For whatever reason, he was a dog of even temperament, sensitive to his handler, sensitive to atmosphere when he was working.

He seemed to be the perfect police dog and, in many ways, he was just that. Yet it was that very sensitivity to atmosphere and to his handler that may have ended his career.

No Ordinary Dog

THERE WAS no indication of distress as Taz and Elaine developed a solid partnership in the North Essex Dog Section. Essex is a large county, the police boundary ending at the south along the Thames from the estuary out past Tilbury Docks, skirting around the eastern edge of London where it meets the boundary of the Met, and extending up to border Hertfordshire, Cambridgeshire and Suffolk. There are several large towns (including Colchester, where Taz and Elaine were stationed, Chelmsford and Basildon, and one city in Southend) and vast expanses of rural land which covers farming and woodland. Unlike the Met and other City-based forces in the Midlands and North, it was possible for a dog handler to find themselves travelling swiftly from an urban incident to the heart of a woodland, alongside the challenge of keeping an animal in sight while they search for anyone who was lost, either by accident or design.

Rural crime centres around farms and around the use of land illegally, which can be anything from a rave to an illegal hunt. The woodlands were also a perfect spot for those who wished to get lost, and to find a private place where they could end their lives. Tracking those who chose to do this was always a grim task, as the majority of these suicides were by hanging. The handler would set the dog to trail a scent into the sometimes dense woodland, which could also be impenetrably dark as the day wore on.

Some police officers are lucky enough to never find a hanging suicide during their time on the job. Elaine was the opposite, and several times Taz led her along a trail until he would stop and look up, having arrived at the end of the scent. Inevitably, she would follow Taz's direction to find the site of a suicide. On one occasion, she was not quick enough to follow Taz's lead and found herself, in the dark, hit in the face by the dangling feet of a victim. These days were some of the grimmest in the job.

Yet despite this, Taz's grounded nature meant that he was able to live at home with Elaine and her family. By this time, her son was enrolling in secondary school and she had a granddaughter who was only a few years old.

'She could lay on Taz's back, lengthways, and he would just lay there and let her,' Elaine described. 'He was a good family dog, able to adjust to working and to standing down. He knew the difference between home and work. But he was not a pet, he was still a working dog, just standing down.

'He didn't become a family pet in the way of most dogs until after his retirement. Despite his grounding, there was always a difference in the way we treated him. He could not, because of the nature of the work he was trained for, be treated as most people would treat their pet dogs: honestly, most owners spoil and indulge their dogs in some manner, and although there was always the temptation to do this, I wouldn't allow it.'

Taz still had a way of showing Elaine how much he thought of her, trusted her, and was bonded to her. It was a small thing that he continued into his later retirement, but it was very indicative of his nature.

'I never allowed him into my bedroom, but I had a small room which I used as a dressing room. He was allowed into that. He liked to go in there when I was there and hide behind the furniture. I'd see his eyes and eyes pop up above the top of a chaise lounge I had in there, or else I'd see his nose poking out at the end. He liked to settle himself but he was also determined to let me know that he was keeping an eye on me.'

Whatever she was doing, Taz was there. He was that close to her.

Taz had been trained as a general purpose dog rather than

as a specialist sniffer dog. This meant that although he could follow trails, he was not trained for specific scents like drugs or explosives (though most general purpose dogs can follow scent trails and sniff out some substances as a matter of course). This meant that much of his training was based around response to command and facing hazards.

Usually at fairly close quarters. The one thing Taz had that many other dogs in Essex did not have at that time was distance training, as it was not something that was taught during the general training course. It had been at one time, but by the time that she had joined the dog section, it had been discontinued. Elaine, however, chose to do this herself just to see if Taz was capable of learning such skills.

She had the measure of Taz. She knew he could go further than most. He had the intelligence, and he responded to her very well. She began to send Taz for some distance and stop him with a command. He would wait. And when her next command came, he would respond to that even if he was 100 or 200 yards away. She also did this in reverse, walking a couple of hundred yards from him while he waited, and then calling. She did this with a verbal command, and also evolved signals which meant that she could do this silently if necessary. Taz was sharp enough to follow these non-verbal commands, even at a distance.

Because it was not part of training, she didn't mention it to anyone, although those who were training with her were aware that she was practising with distance. It was only when the instructor asked at the end of a session if anyone had done any distance training that she was outed: she had no intention of letting on about it, as it wasn't part of the course, but when it was mentioned one of her colleagues thought it might be worth putting her on the spot.

'She can do it,' he said, indicating to Elaine.

'Without having had the training? Prove it,' the instructor challenged, not believing that she had been able to achieve something that was off-curriculum and known to be difficult. Elaine had not wanted to let anyone know that she had been working on this, and was less than pleased with her big-mouthed colleague, especially now that the instructor decided that she would have to put Taz through his paces.

He made her send Taz away a couple of hundred yards and could see that he responded well to her hand signals and to her commands. He then made her put her arms down by her sides so that Taz only had the verbal cues: this was considered the hardest part of distance training, as to respond verbally without any visual cues is difficult for a dog: thinking about how sheepdogs learn, the instruction is always about a mixture of command, whistle and hand gesture.

To the instructor's surprise, Taz responded perfectly to purely verbal commands. Handler and dog once again proving the bond that had built between them. Their greatest strength.

If her colleague's aim had been to see her fail, then it had backfired.

While being deployed with Taz, Elaine also trained with a sniffer dog. If you had a general purpose dog and met the standard and criteria, which was a fairly high bar, then you could apply to train for a specialist dog. Elaine worked with a drugs, cash, weapons and ammunition recovery dog. She was the first woman in Essex to undergo this specific training. And once again she found herself paired with the most difficult dog on the course. She has a photograph of the team she trained with. It became apparent that the more well-built the officer, the smaller the dog they had, mostly Spaniels.

In the middle of the photo is Elaine, with a large Labrador

crossed with a Weimaraner. While this already put her at a physical disadvantage given the relative sizes of officer and dog, this was a boisterous animal that would have been a problem, physically, for any of the officers who handled it.

She had other problems, too, which had more lasting effects.

'All specialist dogs are put on retractable leads because the basis of the role is that the dog is allowed to be free and unhindered at work, and so has no discipline training,' Elaine explains. 'A lead with a lot of length is essential for this. The problem was that my dog's lead was also elasticated. The upshot of this was that when he charged away at speed, the combination of dog and lead would pull my shoulders in all directions. As a result, I ended up with frozen shoulders on the left and the right, and even all these years later I still get stiff and painful shoulders at times.'

Elaine believes that she had the most difficult dog to handle in both general purpose and sniffer dog training. It is unusual to have three dogs in three years, and she feels this may be because she was never first in line for any good dogs that came up.

At times she was ready to quit, but she didn't because this had been her dream, so she simply worked harder, was better, passed everything first time, and didn't complain. At that time there was still a very large amount of sexism in the police force.

It was a good job, then, that she had a dog like Taz at her side. He was able to work in riot and crowd control, he could chase and detain, attack and hold, and search and sniff. He could be used in missing person searches as easily as he could be used for pursuing perpetrators and suspects. He had the sensitivity to adjust and adapt.

TAZ: THE COST OF DUTY

Nightclubbing

TAZ'S ADJUSTMENT skills meant he could prove himself when force was needed. On one occasion, a call came through for a dog and handler to respond to a call from an officer who was having problems with a man thrown out of a club in the middle of Colchester. On call, Elaine and Taz responded.

'It was Friday night. Colchester is a military town and so the weekends can be a busy time as the locals and the squaddies from the nearby base have a lot of steam to let off, some of which is let off at each other. And when you are dealing with the military, that steam can be very violent. For this reason, the Essex Police and the Royal Military Police (RMP) liaise closely and can be seen as a very visible presence around the pubs and clubs in the town centre.'

It's not uncommon for officers to call for back-up, but what Elaine and Taz arrived to find was not quite the usual brawl. It was one man. But no ordinary drunk spoiling for a fight: this man was a bodybuilder, so he had immense upper body strength.

After tangling with the bouncers who had thrown him out of a club and leaving them in his wake, he had decided to take on the police and the RMP officer who had arrived on the scene and were attempting to detain him.

As she arrived with Taz, Elaine could see that both officers had pinned the man down against a car, with one of them hanging on each arm. As if they weighed nothing at all, the man they had pinned down threw them off, sending them sprawling across the road. Seeing the handler and dog in front of him, he made a move towards Elaine.

'By now, Taz was being 'revved up' to attack and hold,' she said, 'as it was obvious that this was what needed to be done…'

She gave the body builder fair warning, 'You calm down and back off, or I'll let him go.'

He just laughed. 'I haven't got a problem with that. Bring it on. Let's see what I can do with him…'

This was to be his downfall. Elaine gave the command and Taz shot towards him, leaping and throwing him back with the impact before he had a chance to move. The dog had him pinned against the car and was holding him by the shoulder. Taz's intelligence was on show as usually dogs are trained to go for the forearm.

This is why the sleeve technique is used in training, this technique being the one where the police officer who is acting the role of perpetrator wears a jacket with padded sleeves, so that when the dog takes the officer down it will not injure them in any way.

But Taz knew that this man had strong forearms and strong biceps, because he had just watched him throw off a military police officer and police officer. Taz was too smart for him. He jumped and pinned him down against the car by his shoulder. He seemed to know that this meant that the arms were now free for them to move in and take the man.

By pinning him at the shoulder, Taz left that arm free for the RMP man to grab, while the other was taken by the police officer. With Taz still holding on, they were able to take the man down, restrain and cuff him until he could be taken to Colchester custody suite.

Once he had been checked in and was in a cell, Elaine had to go and see him. It's a part of procedure that if a dog has attacked someone in the line of duty, then once the detainee has been checked in, the handler is obliged to go and see them, in order to ascertain if any injury, and of what sort, has been inflicted. Elaine would have to make a report on this.

TAZ: THE COST OF DUTY

Sometimes this is straightforward, but more often than that a dog handler will find themselves faced with a recalcitrant and hostile prisoner. Such was the case when she stepped into the cell with the body builder.

'What do you want? I don't want to talk to you,' he started. 'Get out.'

He grumbled and moaned until she patiently explained that it might do him a bit of good to talk to her and let her see what Taz had done when he pinned him down.

'Why should I show you what your dog has done?' he grumbled. 'You want to have a good look at what he can do, then?'

At which Elaine sighed. Not the first time she had heard this. 'It's procedure,' she explained patiently. 'I need to record any wounds that the dog may have inflicted. It's as much for you as anything else, as if you have an insurance claim–'

It was as if she had muttered the magic words: suddenly he became co-operative, if still a little sullen.

'Alright, I suppose you can have a look,' he said and took his shirt off to reveal, on the shoulder that Taz had pinned him by, a large and intricate tattoo of a tiger. Elaine examined the injury and took down all the details for the report. When she was finished, she couldn't resist remarking: 'Looks like my dog got your cat…'

It was only a passing remark, but he took it far from kindly. He started to kick off again, ranting at her about her dog and what he'd done in terms that would look far from complimentary in print.

She left him in the cell to cool off. Even now, years later, the idea that Taz nailed a cat on the body builder's shoulder raises a smile.

First In Line

ANOTHER ASPECT of Taz's training meant that he could also work with armed response units. A dog in this context would enter a situation by going between the legs of the armed police unit. The tactic for a dog in this scenario would be for it to enter a scene to affirm if it was clear and to find a way ahead. If not, the dog would bark and withdraw. The dog is the point man for the operation.

There is however one drawback to this for the armed officers. Some dogs can be hyped up by the situation, 'revved up' as they are by their handlers in order to be at the right pitch for whatever they may face. Some dogs are not very good at this kind of operation, as when excited they can bite. And considering how they enter a situation, it's about where they could bite. As most armed response teams at this time were primarily male, there was an extra worry about the possibility of an over-excited dog nipping where it shouldn't. For this reason they are sometimes a little wary of the dogs that are used.

Taz would keep his head straight down, concentrating on the task ahead. With a focus like a laser beam, he was a dream to work with and the armed response units were always happy when it was Taz that turned up. They knew no-one would get a bitten leg as he passed through the line.

He was also used to helicopters as he'd been deployed in this way more than a few times and so became quite used to being taken up in a helicopter and then leaving it on landing to go about his job. This calm in face of things that many dogs – even those with training – would find a cause for anxiety marked him out as a cut above most. He was also unphased by speed in the back of the van. Elaine had undertaken advanced driver training, as had all the handlers. It was necessary to be able to drive from location to location with speed and safety. After all, there were only ever five officers from the dog section on duty at any one given time, covering the whole of Essex. That's some distance to cover in an emergency needing immediate response. To be a useful handler, you needed that skill. Seven years into his service, Taz was approaching retirement age, but still had a good couple of years' service ahead of him. The dream Elaine had since she was a schoolgirl had come true, and with a dog of exceptional level of intelligence and understanding. What could go wrong?

Collateral Damage

LIFE CHANGED for Taz and Elaine on June 6th, 2011. Although Taz was closing in on retirement, he still had a reputation in the dog section and beyond as a dog you could rely on with absolute certainty. One particular incident would speed up his retirement and affect him in a way that was quite unexpected. It would also have an effect on Elaine that she wouldn't realise for a long time afterwards..

The situation they were called to had been going on for some time. Elaine and Taz were called to a house in Bartram Avenue, Braintree. A man named David Oakes, a former bouncer with a drug problem, was holed up in a house with his partner, Christine Chambers and her two-year-old daughter Shania. Oakes had a history of abusive behaviour towards Chambers, who had separated from him.

There was a restraining order served on him, but he had chosen to ignore this and had left the caravan he was living in to go back to her family home and seek her out. This was not an uncommon pattern of behaviour, for in the two years leading up to this event the police had attended either Oakes' residence or Miss Chambers' address at least six times.

When Elaine and Taz arrived at the scene, they found that the road was deserted and there was an eerie quiet that had fallen over the neighbourhood. The usual sounds of a police presence – radio contact, vehicles, officers talking – were at a remove from the house and immediate street area. Although she had already been told that there was a situation in progress, it was only when she was brought up to speed on what was required from Taz that she understood what was going on. Christine Chambers' older daughter had escaped from the house earlier in the afternoon, after Oakes' arrival, and had made her way to her uncle's where she had raised the alarm. He, in turn, had contacted the police; this was what brought them to the address in the first instance. Attempts to talk to Oakes and to enter the house had escalated the situation to the point where they were now in a potential hostage situation, with no knowledge of what was going on inside.

Outside, a stealth surveillance team were keeping watch, looking for any signs of movement that would give an indication not only of what might be happening, but where in the building it was occurring. The problem the police had if they wanted to enter the house and take Oakes down was simply that they had no clear idea of the layout of the house, and where Oakes had Christine and her daughter. The houses in Bartram Avenue were uniform in their room layout, but it was a question of what those rooms may be used for, and what obstacles may stand between the entrance to the house and where the perpetrator and his hostages were located.

An armed response unit were in place and ready to go. No doubt they were glad to see Taz appear on site. There was no need to worry about a 'revved up' dog starting to nip when he was around. They were certain that Taz would be able to go in and clear the way for them.

Under the direction of the tactical advisor (TA), they waited until daylight before entering the house. The procedure then is straightforward. The dog is sent in ahead of the armed unit, who are standing in front of the handler for protection. The handler sends the dog through the ground floor. If all is clear, the dog comes back. If all is not clear, the dog will either bark or make some signal to indicate that there are people within a room. Once the ground floor is cleared and secured, then the stairs and the first floor are next to be cleared. This process continues until a whole building is secured. In this instance, there were only two floors – ground and first – to be cleared, and if the ground was clear, then the armed response unit would know that their target was confined to the upper floor and could formulate their strategy according to the results of the dog's sweep of the upper.

As they entered the house it was quiet, almost deathly silent. At a signal from the armed response team, Elaine sent Taz in through their legs and into the building. He was gone for a short while, from hall to living room to kitchen and back again. He hadn't made a sound.

The armed response team leader turned back to Elaine. 'Are we clear?'

'Clear,' she confirmed. 'He's been round, and quick.' As Taz had come back without waiting in any room, Elaine presumed it was now clear for the team to enter.

The armed response team were next to sweep the ground floor and confirmed that it was clear. Now they came to the staircase. It was obvious from the state of the stairs that there had been some violent activity. Now that it was so quiet, there was no knowing how this had been resolved, and what was waiting for them up there.

There was a banister rail leading up the stairs. This was on the left, with the landing at the top of the stairs disappearing to the right. The tallest of the firearms team spotted little legs on the floor, jutting out from the right. The rest of the body was out of sight, round the corner on the landing. At first it was thought it was a doll. Or at least, it was hoped that it was: the alternative was unthinkable.

The team leader turned to her again. 'Send him up, clear the first floor.'

The dog would always be sent in ahead: collateral damage, as it was uncertain that Oakes would appear around the corner with a gun and start shooting. The dog would be shot first, giving the team necessary seconds to prepare.

At Elaine's signal, Taz went between the legs of the team and up to the top of the stairs. Then he should have turned right, and been out of sight. But instead of proceeding to check the rooms as he usually would, he stopped. For a moment he was still. And then he reacted in a manner that was completely abnormal, and at the time caused confusion and irritation in the armed response team.

Looking back on that night, Elaine describes his movements at this point as 'being strange and completely out of character'. Usually, Taz would move forward and start with the first room he came to. However, this time, having stopped, he turned his head and looked directly at Elaine. Then he turned his head back and looked straight ahead at what was on the floor in front of him. He then turned his head back to Elaine again. He repeated this several times, looking from what was directly ahead of him down to Elaine and back again. It was like watching a clockwork toy, moving in a rhythmic and definite way. Whatever was going on in his head, he would not go forward as his training would make him – as he always had.

Elaine called him back down, and he came to her. The armed

response team leader was angered and confused, 'What's going on here? What was all that about?'

This was not the way a police dog usually behaved. It was particularly not like the always reliable Taz. She was at a loss to explain this when asked. She managed a reply, 'I don't know. I can't explain it. He's not like him. He's never done this before.'

Even as she was saying it, at the back of her mind she perhaps had a nasty suspicion of what Taz had found. Regardless, this should not have affected him. If it was what she suspected, it was not something that should affect the dog in that manner, not with his training and intelligence. The dogs were trained to be confronted with almost anything, and certainly Taz had encountered a number of dead bodies in the line of work.

She sent Taz up again. Once more, he got to the top of the stairs and then stopped. He turned and looked at her. It was as if he held her gaze before turning to look back to the landing ahead of him once more. He did this several times. Look back, look down. Look back, look down….

He had never been like this before. The first time had been strange enough, but this was more so. It worried Elaine in that it was so out of character, and for what he may have seen to cause this. In answer to the questioning glances she was getting from the armed response team – who were frankly as baffled by Taz's behaviour as she was – she told them, 'I don't know what's going on here, but this is the second time. It's not going to do any good sending him up again. I'm going to have to withdraw him, and you'll have to go ahead and try to clear the upper rooms on your own.'

Obviously, they were far from happy with this outcome, but they had little choice but to proceed and take the upper floor room by room. With Taz recalled and out of their way, the team proceeded up the stairs.

The first thing they found was that the legs they saw from downstairs did not belong to a doll; they were the legs of two-year-old Shania, murdered by Oakes and left lying on the landing. Proceeding into a bedroom they found Christine Chambers dead. She had been tortured and killed by Oakes, who had tried to shoot himself some time before but had made a poor job of it and was now lying semi-conscious on the bed. He had the audacity to ask the armed response team for water.

Oakes recovered from his injuries and the following year stood trial at Chelmsford Crown Court where he was found guilty of double murder and sentenced to a whole life term. Which didn't turn out to be that long as he died shortly afterwards from cancer.

The aftermath for Taz was confusing for Elaine. Those around her were happy to put Taz's behaviour down to just a blip, a one-off in an otherwise exemplary record. The dog section were happy for him to continue on duty. While they may have been content to write this off as simply an anomaly, Elaine could not feel the same way. She wanted him to go back to training so that she could test him. She knew that he had changed. Not just with work, but around the house when they were at home. Taz was different, but it was not something that she could put her finger on. Something had happened to him: his behaviour was different, not in any way she could describe. It was more of a feeling.

Years after the event, Elaine spoke to her son Liam, who was 11 at the time this happened. He confirmed that he always felt Taz was different after that event, that he had changed in some way, and it was really noticeable around the house. It was something that the whole family could see in his behaviour.

Elaine made a request for retraining that was turned down. She was told that it wouldn't be necessary for Taz. The official opinion was that there was nothing wrong with him and he was still able to perform. She pressed again for this and told the dog section that she would need to put him through an exercise in order to be sure that nothing had changed with him, and he would still react as he should in a similar situation. When it counted, could she still rely on him to be his old self? She wasn't so sure, even if everyone else was. The scenario she wanted training to set up for her would be a recreation of what had happened in Bartram Avenue. She felt this was the only way she could be sure.

The trainer she spoke to told her that this would be impossible. Not unreasonable when she came to consider it: how would it be possible to set up a scenario that would exactly reproduce those conditions? It couldn't be done artificially and so would not give a result that really meant anything.

Despite assurances, Elaine felt that Taz could not go on with the job. At the same time, she was also feeling that she needed a change. Looking back at it now, she believes that what she was feeling was the beginnings of PTSD, with which she was later diagnosed. She felt there was no support for her within the force, even the casual support that comes from colleagues.

She told me, 'The problem was that the armed response team could talk amongst themselves about the night's events. But dog handlers – well, we're always alone in the field in that sense. And as we work for the most part alone, we can't even talk it over with other dog handlers.'

What she felt and what she had experienced had no means of expression.

If this was true for Elaine, then so, too, must it have been for Taz. How can a dog, even one with the obvious intelligence of Taz, express what it feels inside when it comes up against a situation that affects it with such force? It's far too easy for those of us who are not in the job to underestimate the trauma that can be suffered from the intense and psychologically scarring events that police officers encounter as part of the job. Is it too much to then assume that service animals can also be affected by some of these things, even if they have been trained to a high degree? Do we underestimate the empathy these animals have?

At the time, Elaine didn't realise what was happening to her. She just knew that she needed to change, even if it meant giving up a job that she had wanted since childhood, and in which she had been fulfilled. It didn't occur to her to question at that point why this lifelong ambition seemed to count for nothing. All she knew was that she wanted out. She moved to the public protection department. No-one asked why she was leaving the section she loved. After a while, she knew she hated the new job. It was only a few years later that she retired.

Her main concern was for Taz. She asked that if she left the dog section, could Taz retire with her? He was now coming up to the age at which police dogs would be retired from working, and if she could get him retired, then he could leave the section with her, and she would not have to give him up. This was something that she could not contemplate, and so it was vital that she get agreement for the dog's retirement. Fortunately, given the concerns that she had herself raised, it was soon agreed that Taz could retire with her.

Elaine went on to do a variety of jobs and Taz became a much-loved family pet. Now free of the demands of being a working dog, they were able to treat him in the manner they wanted. He became spoiled, in a good way, and just as he had been good with Elaine's children, so he went on to be as good with her grandchildren. Indeed, even when he had been a working dog, his grounded nature meant he was good for, and with, children. After all, it was while he was working that

Elaine's granddaughter could lay along Taz's back, using him as a cushion, while he lay on the floor. Perhaps the fact that he was so used to young children may have been part of the reason for what happened to him?

As part of his working duties, he had attended a number of schools and fetes on behalf of the dog section, and he had an affinity for the children he had met through this. He was a smart, empathic dog. This was one of his strengths, but perhaps had that been his Achilles heel on that night? He had not, in his many experiences, ever recovered or found a dead child before. But he had a knowledge of children and their vulnerability, not just from Elaine's granddaughter but from those kids he had met as part of the school visits he had made.

Taz was much more than just a working dog. He was much more than just a pet. He was Elaine's right hand. There was a bond between them. This was established almost immediately and comes only on those rare occasions when you meet a dog that has a complete empathy and bond with you. He was protective towards her and her family. Her daughter described Taz as 'feeling' her mother's pain over what happened. Certainly, his own courage never flagged: even when he was old and his mobility was lessened, he thought nothing of throwing himself down the stairs in order to protect Elaine's daughter, who he knew was frightened by a storm raging outside. Family, his sense of duty and responsibility, came first for him. Always.

Taz eventually passed away at the age of 13. Elaine still has his ashes. In the entrance hall of her home, she has a frame which has a number of photos of Taz with her family, and poems written about him by them. Taz was undoubtedly a huge part of her life. Of their lives. Which is only fitting given his huge personality.

Retirement

TAZ HAD a happy retirement with Elaine, travelling with her and enjoying family life. He was lucky that his handler was able to take him when he left service. Other dogs are not always so fortunate. Handlers whose dogs retire while they are still in the service sometimes live with their handler and the handler's new dog. Sometimes this situation does not work out because of the temperament of the dogs. Sometimes it's just not possible for the handler to take a retired dog.

So, what happens to them then?

When Taz retired, he entered a whole new life as do all retired dogs. He became an ambassador for the Essex Retired Police Dog Fund and attended functions where money was raised. Elaine became, and still is, a trustee of the fund. These bodies are vital for retired dogs because the force they came from cannot pay for the upkeep and maintenance of retired dogs. Indeed, with budget cuts, many police forces, the Met amongst them, have already been talking about possible cuts to their dog sections.

If you consider the case of Essex at the time Taz was active, when you had just five dogs on any shift to cover the whole of the county, then you start to wonder how deep any such cuts can bite. Therefore, the onus is on those who have been handlers, those who have known police dogs, those who have re-homed retired police dogs.

Rehoming a police dog can be one of the best ways in which someone can help. But it doesn't always come cheap or easy; a retired dog may have issues – like Taz – that arise from trauma on the job. They may have injuries from deployment that mean mobility and health need to be taken into account. Some dogs may have been retired because of congenital defects that were only discovered in training, such as problems with legs and joints, deafness, or sight issues.

To help in the maintenance and assistance of retired dogs, there are a number of charities dotted around the country, loosely allied to their local forces. These charities act both as fundraisers for retired police dogs and also as conduits for people who wish to rehome such animals. They have open days in which owners of retired dogs can mix, and former handlers who were unable to keep their dogs can be reunited with them. They fundraise in order to assist owners willing to take on a retired police dog. They help to pay for veterinary bills and medication; for the ongoing treatment of long-term medical conditions, and for any hardships that may be involved with the upkeep of retired dogs.

The National Foundation For Retired Service Animals (NFRSA) cover all animals in service, not just dogs, but its chair – Countess Lady Bathurst – has a particular passion for dogs and has retired service dogs herself. In order to demonstrate how trained they are with the ball, she pointed out to me that one of her dogs – an ex-sniffer – was so obsessed with her ball that 'if I had this ball in one hand, and a steak in the other, she would choose the ball'. Their address is at the end of the book. They fundraise and run open days amongst many other activities.

The Association Of Retired Police Dog Charities is, at the time of writing, chaired by Linda Belgrove, who has an unflagging enthusiasm and love for these dogs. The Association's website is also at the back of this book, and on that site they have a list of website addresses and emails for the Local Retired Police Dog Charities across the country that take care of retired dogs and those who rehome them. They are in Cumbria; Dyffyd-Powys; Essex; West Yorkshire; London (covering

Met and City of London forces); Merseyside; North Wales; Durham; Staffordshire; West Mercia; one for Wiltshire, Avon, Gloucestershire and Somerset; the British Transport Police; and one covering Isle of Wight, Oxon, Bucks & Berks as well as the Thames Valley & Hampshire Police and the Hampshire Fire and Rescue Service.

The charity for Lancashire was founded by a lady named Sheila Maw, who started the charity over two decades ago and is still involved with it now that she is in her 90s.

Sometimes retired police dogs are used for welfare purposes after they leave the service. They can be sent to schools, hospitals, and care homes as well-being or therapy dogs. They are used to promote the force and also at the same time to show that these dogs have a much greater use than some may expect from the standard general purpose dog. Their qualities of empathy and understanding come to the fore, and they have a second life of service as they enjoy their retirement.

Empathy and welfare dogs can be useful within the force. These are dogs with specialist training used for helping to track vulnerable people when they go missing. Perhaps one of the most high-profile dogs used for well-being within the police service is Baloo, a three-legged Malinois who lost one of her legs in the line of duty with Essex Police. She had been featured at Crufts for her achievements and in 2025 was awarded the Kennel Club Hero Dog Award for both her service on duty, her courage, and the work she has entered into after her retirement. The Metropolitan Police was one of the first to welcome well-being and trauma dogs into its service for use by staff and colleagues in 2021. They joined Dexter, who was already in service, in helping colleagues to deal with their mental health.

These dogs need to be sociable, calm, and have an affinity for human interaction, the roles and skills of the handler being vital in this. Their primary role is to support officers who have been subjected to one or possibly several traumatic events or alternatively are suffering from the cumulative effects of their role. This is particularly important for those investigating child exploitation with its exposure to indecent and traumatic images, or other operational roles

There is an organisation called OK9, who have non-policing dogs to support police officers, and which can be used in the community. Its mission statement runs: 'Oscar Kilo, the national police well-being service provides support and guidance for all police forces to improve and build upon well-being within their organisation. Their services have been developed by policing for policing and are designed to meet the unique needs of officers and staff.'

The needs of mental health in staff and indeed in the dogs is something of which the service is now becoming more aware. It was not always this way. Far from it. As we have seen, the way in which dogs are treated by police forces across the country has mirrored the way in which society in general regards their animals. This has changed, and will continue to do so as the way in which the service regards its dogs as working individuals evolves. Their service is now noted and appreciated as never before.

Remarkable and Commended

ANY DOG that serves is worth remembering and being recognised for what they do. Some have careers or individual acts that set them apart, while some are recognised as representative of dogs as a whole.

The PDSA is an organisation that is particularly keen on promoting the use of dogs with the police, as well as with the fire service and as medical assistance dogs. Their order of merit was introduced in 2014 to honour and recognise animals whose bravery, courage and skill had in some way contributed to the continued safety of the public.

Most of these awards go to dogs, including those pets who are invaluable to the continuation of their owners' health or who have shown incredible acts of courage – although not a police dog, mention must be made of Oi, the Adshead family dog who protected her owners when masked thieves burst into their home in 2008. They wielded machetes and the unheeding Oi attacked and bit one of them on the hand. Despite being struck on the head twice, the dog then chased them out of the house and down the street. Her wounds were bad enough to require emergency surgery, but she thankfully recovered. Although not a police dog, her courage and loyalty show the qualities that make dogs such an important part of policing. Her deserved award came retrospectively.

Another one of their notable awards was to a Springer Spaniel called Charlie, whose ability to find a murder victim buried in a large field contributed to a conviction in 2008. This was just a small part of his long career, during which he was also responsible for locating an elderly and vulnerable old lady who had been in the open for over 14 hours in freezing weather. His discovery saved her from a certain death by exposure. He found a dementia patient who had gone missing and was bogged down in mud, preventing her from drowning. His work extended to representing search and rescue dogs in the House of Lords and the recruitment and training of other dogs for specialist forces. He was sent with his handler to Ascension Island in the South Atlantic in a missing persons search, along with two blood detection dogs. They searched through brutal terrain in terrible weather conditions, and although they found nothing, this did confirm that the search could be closed and attention focused elsewhere: always an important part of the job.

Returning home, and showing another facet of the job, Charlie's search of a fire-damaged and unsafe building where one body had been recovered confirmed that there were no others, and allowed demolition to proceed. In his later years, Charlie was retired with the family of Robyn Smith, and found himself in the news when he broke his leg colliding with a police dog while chasing a ball.

Robyn told reporters, 'Charlie loves retirement and has grown really affectionate. He loves cuddles and snoozing on his many comfy beds. He's still ball-obsessed and will try to outrun much younger dogs to get to the ball first. He doesn't act his age! Last month, Charlie was playing with his ball when he ran into a bigger dog, injuring his leg. Charlie already had a weak front leg from his years of service, and when we adopted him we were told he had arthritis. He's a tough boy who doesn't show his pain, but after colliding with the other dog he was clearly in pain, so we rushed him to the vet.'

Vets discovered that Charlie had previously suffered a mild fracture which had been there for years and had weakened over time, so when he hurt himself playing the impact caused a severe break. Charlie ended up with a metal plate and five screws, along with a frustrating period of crate rest during his recovery, but went on to continue his happy and deserved retirement.

Jake was another award winning Springer Spaniel who served with Warwickshire Police for a career of over 10 years, which is in itself remarkable. His operational finds as a sniffer include assault rifles, shotguns and handguns, £650,000 worth of banknotes and £4.5 million in illegal drugs. His handler

PC Andy Crouch had him from 18 months old, when he underwent his first drugs search course. Further courses for firearms, ammunition, and banknotes. He worked the Cheltenham Gold Cup and the Glastonbury Festival as well as other music events.

One time he leaped through the open window of a car to uncover £1,000 worth of cocaine hidden under the central console. Another time, he found £2,000 worth of cannabis hidden on a tour bus which meant a delay before the headlining act could deal with the police and get themselves on stage.

Sniffer dogs are a different kind of dog to the general purpose dog: they all have personalities that make them unique, but the sniffer dog's duties mean that it leads a very different working life. It can be a little less rigid in its behaviour, and a little more eccentric. Or, in the case of some dogs, very eccentric.

There are great working dogs, and there are great working dogs that just impress themselves on everyone they encounter.

Zippy: Sniffing And Snapping

The Legend And The Reality

IN THE introduction, a dog handler was quoted as saying 'it's not the breed of the dog that matters, it's whether or not they can do the job'. That handler was Tony Mayo, and his reason for saying that is rooted in the unique character and breed of the dog he handled for a number of years.

Zippy was a complete anomaly. He came by a roundabout route. He was not a breed that usually gets considered for police work and he had a temperament that was feared across Essex, where he worked. Despite this, Zippy turned out to be the best sniffer in town, featured on TV in 'Police Interceptors' and in police posters of dogs at work.

Zippy was the kind of dog that myths and legends grow around. A towering presence for a tiny dog. When I first heard about him, the story ran that Tony discovered him as a pup when he was visiting a traveller site for another call. He rescued the dog and took him to a vet. Checking him over, he saw something in the dog that made him want to take him on and see if he could be trained. Zippy formed an immediate bond with Tony that was, to say the least, unique. Zippy adored him and would snap at anyone else – an attitude summed up to me by someone who knew them as 'kill 'em all, except Tony'.

It's a cracking story, but sadly it's not quite true, although the legend did amuse Tony when I asked him about it. The truth is a little more prosaic, but nonetheless remarkable, and takes nothing away from what happened once Tony and Zippy were a team. In many ways, the real story is no less incredible.

'That's not how it happened,' Tony told me. 'Zippy was recovered as a young dog from Harlow where he was seized alongside two siblings. The vet estimated that he was about 17 months at the time. All three were taken because of neglect and were not in the best of health when they were brought to the kennels. As fox terriers, they were probably bred for their hunting ability as there were reports of illegal hare coursing, fights and hunts across more rural parts of Essex. Traveller sites are well-known for having large numbers of such dogs running wild. Of course, I didn't know all this until Vera told me.'

At that time, police dogs in Essex were not bred specifically for the job, but tended to be recruited from those waifs and strays who were donated or found in kennels. In the same kennel, police would also leave those dogs picked up in the course of duty. It's still used for this but has changed hands and name since the days when it was run by an old lady named Vera, who had been there longer than any serving officer could recall, and was a shrewd judge of a dog.

She noticed that one of the three dogs brought in was faster than the rest, stronger too, and showed a real desire to be first to a ball when she played with them. She concentrated on this ball play with the fast little terrier and, because he was always here, there and everywhere, faster than the rest, she named him Zippy. 'Because always zipping about,' she told Tony.

Sniffer dog training, as we have seen, has always been more reliant on ball play and the desire for the ball. Tony explained,

'The desire and drive for the ball is what powers any sniffer dog to be better at their task – if they want it all the time, they will respond to training and be faster than the rest on the job. In Vera's opinion, which you never doubted, Zippy was a natural. All he needed was a handler to go into training with. I didn't know that would be me.'

Tony had been a police officer for a few years and had later joined the dog section, undergoing training with a general-purpose Alsatian named Storm. Having settled into his dog section post, covering South Essex, he was now looking to undergo sniffer dog training. All he needed was to be matched with a dog. So, he was pleased to get a call from the training unit to say that there was a dog ready for him at the kennels.

'I asked him what kind of a dog it was, and he wouldn't tell me at first. He was being evasive, but when I kept on, he asked me if I knew what a fox terrier was. I'd been expecting a spaniel as they were usually what you had as a sniffer, so I said I thought I knew what one was. I wasn't too sure, to be honest.

'When I got to the kennels, they sent me down to what looked like an empty pen. There was no dog in sight. Then, when I got to the door, this little red and white thing started jumping up at me, and I thought "oh no, come on…".'

It was only then, when this small red and white ball of energy started jumping up and barking at him that he realised that this was what a fox terrier looked like. All he could think of at that moment was how he would look turning up at training with what looked like a pint-sized dog next to the others. Fox terriers are small dogs, bred for hunting and getting into tight spots and down burrows. There are two kinds of fox terrier, the smooth coated and the wire haired. Zippy fell into the latter category, with dark eyes blazing out of a face full of fur, his tough little frame covered with what looked like wiry wool that could never be tamed. It suited his rough and ready character.

Turning up at training, it caused the kind of hilarity that Tony had envisaged: all the other handlers had spaniels or labradors, while in the middle of it was this pint-sized ragamuffin who quickly showed that he had an attitude to everyone and everything. Everyone except Tony, that is, as from the moment he saw him, and despite the bemusement with which his presence had been greeted, Zippy had decided that Tony was his human, and the rest of them didn't matter.

And that wasn't all. 'The laughing soon stopped when training started and Zippy showed that his speed and desire for a ball was matched only by how quick and smart he was in picking up the tasks he was being trained for,' Tony recalled.

Small, fast and intelligent, he soon proved his worth and they passed training with ease. Zippy may not have seemed the most intimidating name for a police dog – thinking about it, Tony must have cut an odd figure with Storm at one side, and Zippy on the other – but it suited him. Vera had been right about him in every way.

'I could have changed his name,' Tony said. 'Other handlers sometimes changed the names of their dogs, but somehow Zippy suited the little feller. He had other names and nicknames, but they were all the same sort of thing - Zipster, Mr Zips, and just Zip. He was just him, really.'

Whatever you called him, it was trouble for you unless he was on the job, or you were his beloved Tony. Zippy may have been a small dog, but he was tough. He had to be, as growing up on a traveller site he ran with a lot of other dogs in a pack, some of them much larger than him, so he had to fight his corner all the time.

Tony told me, 'You always see packs of dogs running around,

left to their own devices. So, a little dog, a fox terrier like Zippy would have to be harder than any of the bigger dogs to survive. That's got to be where it came from.'

This attitude was something he continued to carry with him all the way through his life. Whenever he was confronted by larger dogs, either in training or just when he was out on the streets, doing his job and walking around cars, he had a way of carrying himself. Tony remembered that 'he would puff his chest out and give a little growl. It was his way of giving a warning to other dogs, saying I'm here, and I can't be messed with.'

Assert Yourself In The Workplace, Zippy Style

AFTER A while, Tony would play up to the way Zippy was regarded. When he would turn up for a job in the first year or two of Zippy's career, other officers who were not from the dog section would look at him askance.

'They'd look at him like they were thinking "Really? That's a police dog?". I didn't like that.' As a result, Tony got quite protective of him. After a while, as the other officers got used to him, they would just take him as he was. But that didn't mean that their earlier attitude was forgotten.

Because Zippy was small, he looked cute. 'So, all these other officers would sometimes ask me if they could give him a stroke. They'd want to make a fuss of him as he looked really sweet. I'd say to them sure, why not, it's fine. By all means, make a fuss of him. And he would let them come near…'

Now, the reason Zippy looked so sweet was partly because of the way that Tony used to carry him around. Those of us of a certain age may remember the ventriloquist Bob Carolgees and his dog Spit that he used to carry on his arm. Tony got into the habit of carrying Zippy in this way so that he would be seated in the crook of his elbow, which made him look exactly like the way Bob Carolgees held Spit. Given that Spit was a small, scruffy terrier in appearance, the resemblance must have been uncanny. The only difference between them being that while the puppet Spit was black with a touch of grey, Zippy was red and white.

In the same way that Spit would snap at people when they went near him, so when someone would put their hand out to Zippy and he would growl and try and bite. It still raises a smile when Tony recalls the way it would go.

'I used to enjoy this. I'd say, "put your hand out, let him smell it, let him just have a sniff at you…" As they did, he'd look up at me as if to say, "Are we really doing this again?" And I'd look at him and think, oh yes, we are. Let them learn.'

As you might expect, Zippy was a fearless dog, except for one thing. As part of his training, Tony had tested him with many objects, noises and sounds. The one thing that Zippy did not take to was having glass bottles thrown and shattering near him. 'Nothing ever used to get to him, and then one day in training there was a bottle that got smashed, and it made him jump and get nervy. I reckon it was something that happened to him when he was a pup and it was something that still spooked him.'

If he had been a general-purpose dog, then this kind of fear would have been a problem. A general-purpose dog would be likely to come up against the sound of breaking glass and risk having bottles thrown at them in a crowd-control situation. But as a specialist sniffer dog, it didn't really present any problems as he was unlikely to come up against any situation where he would have to face anything of the like thrown in his direction.

Aside from this one issue, Zippy was fearless and had a

tendency to be very much his own dog. It wasn't a matter of discipline when they were out in the field: more a matter of when it was done, Zippy had his own ideas. A perfect example of this comes from when Zippy and Tony were first paired.

'I was based in South Woodham Ferrers at the time, and there's a bridle path that runs down along one side of the police station. After we'd finished a night shift, I liked to let Zippy have a run off the lead along the path, as he had been cramped up in the van for most of the shift and so this gave him some exercise, gave him a chance to loosen up. Usually, he'd have a little run about and it was no problem. But one morning I let him go and that was it: he was off. He ran down the path at full pelt, past some gardens, turned a corner and just disappeared out of sight. I went after him, but he was away and the further down the path you went, the further you strayed into dense woodland.'

After searching for between 45 minutes and an hour with no luck, Tony was starting to feel that he would need some help in locating his missing dog. By chance, there was a helicopter coming back from a job at this time, and somewhat shame-facedly Tony contacted them and asked them if they could have a quick look in the large, wooded area at the back of the station for Zippy. It's easy to imagine how a request from a dog handler to look for his dog would be received. 'They thought it was funny. Probably because I had to ask them about my own dog.' Amidst such amusement, the helicopter took off.

It took some time and the clock was now creeping around to seven o'clock in the morning before the helicopter crew finally located Zippy. Tony was laughing when he told me. 'He'd found a large pond in the middle of the wooded area, and had swum out to the middle. He was now standing on a raised island, having reached his goal, and thoroughly enjoyed himself. As the helicopter was hovering overhead, the crew watched while Zippy would dive in, have a swim, pull himself out, launch himself in again, and keep on doing this. He looked like he could carry on all morning. And they're telling me this over the radio and laughing while they do it.'

Having reported Zippy's position to Tony, the helicopter crew left him to it. Perhaps that was just as well, because when he eventually reached the pond, Tony had to wade in and pull Zippy out. 'He was filthy, covered in all kinds of weed and muck. He had to have a bath. More than one, to get all that off. And he managed to cost Essex police five or six grams worth of helicopter fuel, just because he decided to go for a little run.'

Zippy And Storm: Love And Hate

ZIPPY GOT on well with Storm, Tony's general-purpose dog. Perhaps a bit too well. When it came to putting them both in the van for work, it soon became apparent that although Zippy had been neutered, he still had amorous intentions towards Storm. So much so that he would try to mount him when they were in the back of the van. It was a sight that would take you aback to open the back of the van and find Zippy behind the larger dog, gamely trying to achieve what nature was telling him, even if he wasn't sure why he was doing this given his lack of equipment. Storm tolerated this. When Storm retired and was replaced by Kane, Zippy thought it would be business as usual…

'The first time out he tried to mount Kane in the back of the van just like he had with Storm. Kane wasn't like Storm, and he was having none of it. He turned on Zippy and had a right go at him, putting him in his place. After this, Zippy would get into the back of the van and, leaving Kane alone, go into the corner and face the side of the van, looking away from Kane, just like a naughty kid sent to stand in the corner of the room.'

Storm may have put up with Zippy's advances, and tolerated his love of playing hard and rough when they were in Tony's garden, but he drew the line at Zippy trying to get his nose in someone else's food bowl, as Tony discovered when he heard a yowling commotion in his garage one Christmas Eve.

'I went on to see what the noise was about, and there was Zippy, running around in circles while there was blood all over the walls. The splatter pattern looked just like a wounded bird had been let loose to flutter wildly. I couldn't work out what was going on until I got hold of him and found the side of his head was drenched in blood. A quick visit to the vet was in order, and she discovered that the tip of Zippy's ear had been nipped off by Storm, probably because of a fight over their food bowls. Zip had a habit of sticking his nose in there.'

Anyone who has ever nicked their ear while shaving or cutting hair will know how even the slightest cut there will bleed profusely. It was no wonder the garage looked like a bloodbath.

Zippy recovered. It was not the easiest Christmas Eve Tony ever had, but maybe less so for Zippy as he had a loathing of vets that made any trip difficult for his long-suffering handler. In a working life where a dog may expect to risk injury in the line of duty, Zippy had two injuries incurred – neither of them in the line of work. This was the first. The second, which came later, also highlights his deep distrust and dislike of the veterinary profession.

Work Is Another Matter Entirely...

DESPITE THESE little quirks of behaviour, Zippy turned out to be one of the best search dogs in the Essex force. He was good simply because he was determined. Whatever Tony would throw at him, he would keep going until he could find something. For such a scruffy looking, volatile ball of fur he was a focused little worker. Little being important, as his size was something that counted in his favour.

In house searches, he could do things that other sniffer dogs couldn't. For instance, when you get to the bedrooms in a house search, you could find a whole manner of cupboards and shelving, often with tight, constricted spaces. These would be quite difficult for larger dogs to get into, but for Zippy this presented no problem.

'Small cupboards he could nose his way into, and for shelves I would simply lift him up onto the shelf and let him walk along. The same for the tops of cupboards – just lift him up and he could sniff around up there,' Tony explained.

This was the thing about Zippy that set him apart from other sniffers. This was what was special about him: his size. The same thing that had made some so dubious about him meant that Tony could just literally pick him up and run him along any spaces that were small and otherwise inaccessible. You can't do that with even the smallest spaniel. It was something that Zippy took to with no problem and it was not something that Tony had worked on with him in training. It's not regular for sniffer dogs to be trained in such a manner, but by taking advantage of his size, Tony was able to place him where other dogs would not fit, and Zippy's own instinct and aptitude for the job would take over.

This was an important distinction at a time when the force relied mostly on spaniels and labradors as sniffer dogs. A dog such as Zippy, of which there are still very few in terms of size, had an advantage that proved his worth. Tony felt that because he was 'just some sort of mutt' he was often overlooked because he wasn't of a particular breed. However, his ability in the job overcame everything.

A perfect example of this is a job that Tony and Zippy undertook after there had been a theft of guns and live ammunition from a gunsmith. A few weeks after this, there began a spate of armed robberies around the South Essex area. It was believed that the weapons involved were some of those taken from the gunsmith, and this was likely the reason for their theft. They were now being used to rob petrol stations in the area. The robbers then widened their sphere of operations and decided to rob an Indian restaurant. During this raid one of the guns was discharged and things became a bit more serious as the weapons were no longer just for show.

The perpetrators were not going to stop just because the attempts to catch them had ramped up: they continued to hit petrol stations, and showed themselves not to be the sharpest tools in the shed as they were caught on CCTV using their own vehicle, which still had its original registration. Whether this was stupidity or the sheer arrogance of believing they would not be caught is open to question. Whatever the reason, they were hiding in plain sight and assumed that the vehicle details would not be followed up. It wasn't too long before CID had the men involved in detention.

The problem was that they still hadn't recovered the guns or ammunition, and the clock was ticking. The suspects were being held under caution and the 48 hours custody would soon be up. CID were working against the clock, and their only hope was the knowledge that these men had a lock-up. What was needed was an urgent search. A warrant was obtained, and they called out the dog section.

When Tony and Zippy arrived, they found that the lock-up was a grim, dark warehouse. Their job was to go through the property and see if they could turn up anything that would be useful.

'In the main room of the lock-up, we came up with nothing,' Tony recalled. 'It was like a small factory unit used for engineering, and there were some pieces of machinery and metal engineering tools and materials stored there, but nothing that yielded any kind of result. It was looking pretty much like the lock-up would be a bust. But down at one end there was another smaller room. It was dimly lit and looked like it hadn't been in use, but nonetheless it still needed to be searched. When we got down there, it looked about as useful as the main room. It was empty apart from a pallet that had a few old paint pots standing on it. But as it was the only room left, and the only space where he might find anything at all, I still let Zip have a go around it.

'Slowly, he started working his way around the room. He took his time. He always did. But he found nothing on the walls, nothing on any shelves. I could see they looked empty, but there was always the hope of any trace of a scent that could set him off. Then, when it looked like it was a bust, he reached the pallet at the end of the room. He suddenly stopped dead, then started nosing at it. I couldn't see at first how he could have found anything, but he would not leave it alone. I knew he was on to something, but God knows what.'

Getting down on the floor of the lock-up, Tony looked under the pallet at where Zippy had his nose. A pallet is generally made up of a top and bottom of planks, with a space between them supported by stanchions. This was where Zippy was looking, and whatever he could sniff in there, he was definitely interested. Usually, when a sniffer dog finds something, it will just stand and stare to indicate where its find is located. However, Zippy did not do this.

'He was really excited, trying to get his nose past me and push himself into the space between the stanchions. I tried to distract him with his ball as this usually worked, but he wouldn't leave it alone.'

The ball reward is a usual move for a handler who is trying to get a dog away from an area or rewarding it for what it's discovered. Tony found that Zippy was ignoring the ball, which made him all the more certain he was onto something.

It's an interesting fact that people who are trying to hide something will often try and disguise scents by the places they hide these things, hoping that the other scents around will distract a dog's nose, or mask what they are trying to secrete. They think that it must be easy to fool a dog if you can just mask a scent.

It's not that easy at all, as the men in custody, watching the clock tick down and thinking they just had to sit it out until they were reluctantly released, were about to find out.

Back in the lock-up, no matter how much Tony tried to distract him, Zippy would not stop sniffing around this pallet. Already down on his knees, he pushed the dog out of the way so that he could see under the pallet without Zippy's muzzle obscuring his view.

'I could see it in the cutout of the pallet - something wrapped up. I had gloves on to avoid contaminating it, and very carefully prised it out of the gap. It was wrapped in a cloth, but as I got it out, you could see that it was a shotgun, complete with ammunition, carefully wrapped.'

The shotgun and ammunition were identified as being part of the stolen gunsmith haul, and the same ones being used in the robberies. It was the necessary evidence to further detain the men, who were then charged.

In itself it was a good find, but the key thing about it is that Zippy was actually able to find the gun and ammunition – being made of metal, these are usually the hardest things for any sniffer to detect. A gun and ammunition shells do not carry much scent. Perhaps if they have been fired or cleaned recently then they may carry some residue of scent, but in the case of this shotgun it had been some days since it had last been discharged in the Indian restaurant.

'Drugs have a set of very definite smells that the dog is trained in,' Tony said. 'Cash carries scent from all the people that have handled it as well as from the ink and the paper. To find a gun in this way shows not just an incredible nose, but also a similar tenacity – nice word for stubborn, which he was – from Zip. He was a dog who didn't like to be beaten by anything.'

It turned out to be more than just an excellent result for Tony and Zippy, too, as the men concerned ended up with 11-year sentences for their robbery spree.

An Unlikely TV Star

ZIPPY'S CHARACTER and his ability to find things that might defeat other dogs meant that when a production company started filming the 'Police Interceptors' reality TV series in Essex, he was a natural fit for it. There's one excellent piece of film that sums up Zippy in a few short minutes.

It's night time and a plainclothes officer has pulled over a car which he suspects of carrying drugs. A dog handler was called to have a sniff around the car and its occupants, and Tony and Zippy answered the call. The occupants are standing outside the car and have been searched with nothing found. The car itself has been searched and again nothing has turned up. Reluctantly, the police are about to let them go when Zippy starts to sniff and scratch at the underneath of the car. While the two occupants shuffle around looking a bit sheepish, the uniformed officers get enthusiastic. It's obvious that Zippy is on to something, and it's not long before Tony is down flat on his stomach, looking under the car. Right underneath, dead centre and hard to get at, there is a small bag of what can only be an illegal substance.

After some scrambling under the car to get at the bag, Tony comes up with what is identified as a small bag, but a large wrap of cocaine. Satisfied with this result, Tony tosses the ball to a happy Zippy and the wrap to the plainclothes officer, who is more than pleased at this outcome after what appeared to be a dead end. He's so pleased about this that he asks Tony if he can give Zippy a little pat and fuss... obviously he must have been one of the few officers in Essex who was unaware of Zippy's reputation. Tony tells him that of course he can, and the next thing that camera catches is Zippy snarl and snap at him, trying to take his hand off for daring to try and touch him. Tony and his fellow uniformed officer find this highly amusing. The plainclothes man looks slightly embarrassed at being caught this way, as if knowing that this will haunt him whenever it turns up on TV somewhere.

The voice over used in the piece is very keen to talk about the way police use technology and the amount that was used in this chase. All the while, the occupants of the car are quite happy to stand there looking for all the world as though they will be able to drive away shortly. Meanwhile, as the voice over praises the tech that is used by the police, your eyes are drawn to this scruffy little mutt who won't stop sniffing under the car and trying to scramble underneath, prompting Tony to drop down and have a look.

The lesson here is that technology is all very well, but at the end of the day you can't beat the human – or in this case canine – touch.

A few years after this, our plainclothes man, had another

encounter with Tony and his dog. This time it was Kane, the general-purpose dog that was paired with Tony after Storm was retired. All three of them were involved in a car chase and once they left the cars and the chase continued on foot, the officer once again showed he was not very dog savvy.

'As they got out of the car and legged it, I set the dog after them to chase and detain. Kane was in pursuit when this feller decided that he would be able to outrun the dog. The ridiculous thing was that they had run into a dead end, so Kane would be able to deal with them easily. I'd already shouted out to the other officers to leave it and let the dog do his work when I saw this feller belt past me, and then he was surprised when he found himself brought down by Kane, who assumed that he was just another one of the perpetrators.

All he saw was four blokes running past him now, instead of three. All it meant for the copper was that instead of being in on the arrest, he ended up with a bite on the backside so bad we had to take him to A&E in the back of a police car, sitting on a plastic bag because of the amount of blood that was pouring from the bite. This is not what anyone needs in the middle of an arrest.

'Something good did come out of it, though, in that Essex police changed their defensive skills programme for officers so that it now includes the advice that you don't run in front of police dogs when they are in pursuit, as all you will do is confuse them.'

It is ironic that this change was caused by one officer being bitten by two separate dogs who had the same handler. Possibly, he gave Tony a wide berth after this...

Small Dog Syndrome Has Its Good Points

ZIPPY'S HABIT of biting people gained him quite a reputation. It partly comes from his early upbringing where he had to learn to look after himself pretty quickly amongst the larger dogs and kids where he grew up. And it partly comes from the fact that the officers in the dog section like to let him have a run about and chase trainers who were acting the part of perpetrators, wearing protective sleeves.

This part of training has never really changed: in the exercise, a dog that has been trying to take down someone who is either running away from them or trying to attack them is trained to go for the arm. This is why the sleeve on its own may not always be a good idea – looking at Surrey's training methods in the 1950s, they played it safe and had a fully padded suit for their trainers, which has its benefits.

Well, it seemed to Tony – and the other handlers – that all the other dogs in the section were always getting a chance to have a go at this. And it seemed just so unfair that Zippy should be left out just because he was a sniffer dog, and because he was small.

They liked to let him have a go at the chase, and he took to this perhaps a little too well. He enjoyed the chase and the chance to get stuck in, as it suited his combative nature. Perhaps this didn't help with his general propensity to want to have a snap at people. Particularly other police officers: they were inclined to get a bit too familiar in his opinion, or so it seemed, and they needed to remember their place.

Any police dog may find themselves on the receiving end of aggression from a suspect, and they have to be able to look after themselves. Being small, Zippy could easily be taken for being more vulnerable than most. So, his 'independent' nature was more of an asset than it may first appear.

Small Dog, Big Personality, Bigger Talent

ZIPPY LOVED his work, and he was damn good at it. As he showed on many occasions, sometimes turning up things that were unexpected of him, and were not what he had originally been dispatched to find.

Often, as part of their duties, the dog section would find themselves dispatched to Tilbury Pool, down on the Thames Estuary. This is where all the large container ships come into dock. There are not as many as there used to be now that the super containers demand docking so large they end up partially unloading off the coast of Ireland; neither are there the proliferation of ships that used to flow through Tilbury on their way to the London Docks more than half a century ago. But it's still the main gateway to the Port of London and so has enough trade to warrant attempts at smuggling all kinds of goods.

Intelligence had come in that there was a Russian ship docking, and on board would be machine gun parts that were being smuggled into the country. So, as part of this investigation, the dog team was sent down in order to try and sniff out anything that might be hidden aboard the ship. While this search took place, the ship was shut down, with the crew confined to their cabins as the dogs searched. Tony remembers that 'the cabins themselves were small, poky rooms with a bed that was set in a cut metal structure, with drawers underneath the bed which were mostly used for spare bedding on the voyage. We'd learned this from the searches that had so far turned up nothing'.

With the crew members confined to their cabins, the search in an already confined space was difficult at best. While the cabin was searched, the crew member would be asked to leave the room and wait in the corridor outside.

'There was a cabin that had been difficult from the start,'

Tony recalled. 'The sailor whose cabin it was had not wanted to move out, and he was hostile and argumentative. In a language I didn't understand either as he was Russian and didn't speak any English. He was a big bloke as well.

'I was standing across the doorway with my arm up to block it. I didn't want him to come out of the cabin into the corridor – where there was more room for a fight – until he had calmed down.'

Tony is a big feller, but this sailor was just as big, if not more so. But even with the language barrier, Tony could see that: 'part of the reason this lad was kicking off was because he didn't want to come out and let the dog get on with his job'.

This was an interesting situation. If the general technique was to clear the room of anyone, and this man did not want to come out, how was Tony to persuade him to come out and yet also calm him down? Especially as Zippy had gone in regardless, and was now not only sniffing at one of the drawers, but pawing at it, giving Tony the clear message that he wanted it open. The first thing was to deal with a sailor throwing his arms around in a confined space and shouting very loudly in Russian. Tony had no idea what the Russian was shouting at him, but the general meaning was clear enough: he didn't want the room searched.

'Eventually, I got him calmed down enough so that I could coax him into leaving, still muttering something probably uncomplimentary and insulting. But as he pushed past me, he kept looking back over his shoulder, and he was acting suspiciously. That doesn't change, no matter what language you're speaking. There was definitely something hidden in that drawer under the bunk, as Zippy was not letting up.

'The first thing that I could think of was that some of the gun parts were being stashed in here. If that was the case, then was this sailor armed? We hadn't had to search him.' He got assistance and had the sailor removed to a safe distance. With the sailor secured, Tony got down and pulled the drawer out. 'At first glance, all seemed as you would expect. The sheets that were in the drawer were neatly folded and packed in tightly. There didn't seem to be any room for the gun parts to be there. Whatever Zippy had found, it wasn't that. But whatever it was, he wouldn't stop, and he got stuck into nosing between the tightly-packed sheets.'

As Tony pulled out the sheets and they unravelled, it became clear why the Russian had been so keen for them not to search his cabin.

'The folds between the sheets held a large number of currency notes from across the world, all carefully folded in to prevent them being easily found. The reason the sailor had been so keen to hide them, and keep them that way, was because the law dictates that sailors can only carry a certain amount of currency on board travelling from port to port. This bloke had other ideas and had probably been getting away with it for some time. The last thing he had expected was to come up against a dog as stubborn with his job as Zippy.'

It was not what the police had been looking for, but none-theless an arrest had to be made as a law was broken. For this Russian, the voyage was over.

Tony said, 'To be honest, I felt a little sorry for the sailor when the arrest was made, as the call out had been for something else entirely, and he was just unlucky enough to be in the wrong place at the wrong time. Mind you, he had been overly aggres-sive, and this had come back to bite him. Literally. He'd been in my face so much that while I was trying to calm him down, Zip had left his search and started barking at the sailor, having a bite at him for daring to try and threaten me.'

He was a fiercely loyal little terrier, with the emphasis very much on the fierce.

Probably the best example of this comes from a time when they were called out to another house search. It was a known site for drug use and dealing, and so a raid was not an uncommon occurrence. This time, it was on Tony and Zippy's rota, and so they were the sniffer team who had the pleasure of combing the property. It was pretty much what you might expect from such a place, being run down with little in the way of any housework being done. The occupants had much better ways – in their view – to pass their time. As well as the search for drugs, the police were also after any cash that may be there, and they also had intel that there were stolen goods on the premises.

As part of the search, they came to the small front room of the house where the tenant was lying on the couch with a duvet covering him. As the tenant, he was a prime suspect for any activity that was going down, and as might be expected he was not in the mood to be co-operative. He was distinctly unfriendly.

'We're going to search this room now, so you need to move please,' Tony informed him.

'Why should I? I live here, you're just intruding,' he answered.

'Yeah, but with a search warrant, so really you don't actually have a choice,' Tony replied. The room needed to be searched to ascertain that there were no needles, drugs, or anything else illicit in there.

Obviously, the man, still under his duvet and in no hurry to move, felt that this was an infringement of his human rights.

'I suppose I'll have to let you,' he said grudgingly. It was then that he caught sight of Zippy, and his recalcitrant attitude turned to outright anger. He started to shout and gesture

CANINE CRIMEBUSTERS

towards the dog. Tony can remember his words even now: 'What is that? What's that scruffy little c**t doing in my house? Get him out.'

The irony of a man in a drug den laying under a duvet in the middle of the day referring to Zippy in this way was lost on him with a stunning lack of self-awareness. It wasn't lost on Tony, but it also wasn't the thing that riled him most. Zippy might have been the opposite of what most people would think of as a sniffer dog, but he was Tony's dog, and no-one was going to talk to him like that. Zippy's loyalty cut both ways, after all.

Knowing that Zippy would not react well to being shouted at in that manner and would get narked at the aggression being directed towards him, Tony let him slip off the loop on what had previously been a tight lead. He made it look like an accident, but he knew exactly what he was doing.

The next thing that anyone in the room knew, Zippy had jumped up on the couch and was standing on the duvet, on the man's chest, growling in his face and giving him what for. The man cowered under the duvet, terrified as this angry ball of red and white fur got stuck in.

'Get this little c**t off me, get him off,' he yelled. 'The little c**t is biting me. I'll have you for this…' After which it became less coherent. He continued to yell at Tony to get the dog off him, repeatedly screaming that Zippy was biting him.

He wasn't: he was growling and barking too much to take a chunk out of the frightened suspect. He didn't need to actually sink his teeth in, the man had been taught his lesson, and Tony got Zippy back on the floor so that he could proceed with his job. Which he did very well, as usual, leading to a conviction.

248

Bangers And Banned

STANSTEAD AIRPORT, now London's third largest airport in terms of traffic, comes under the purview of the Essex police and was a place where dog handlers and sniffer dogs were often called out to perform searches. It's possibly a badge of honour that Zippy managed to get himself banned from the airport. In fact, he may well be the only police dog to get himself banned from anywhere in such a manner…

At one time, the dog section carried out a large number of different operations at the airport, partly to do with the law regarding the amount of cash that can be brought into a country, and partly to do with searches for smuggled drugs. Stanstead brings in a lot of traffic from Eastern Europe and it was this traffic that was, at one time, most associated with the influx of illegal cash. Because of this, the local police team would conduct a large number of random searches. Often, they would call a dog unit from Essex to come and assist the locals and the airport security.

On this particular day, the airport team were having some issues with a Spanish passenger who had just arrived and was being detained pending a search. They wanted a sniffer to have a look over the man's luggage and the team on call that day was Tony and Zippy. When they arrived at the airport they found that the Spanish passenger's suitcase had been opened and was laying there on the floor waiting for Zippy to do his bit: there was also a laptop sitting in the suitcase.

'Would you have any objection, sir, to my dog searching through your case?' Tony asked the passenger politely. It wasn't as if he actually had a choice, but he agreed anyway.

'I suppose so,' he said reluctantly, 'but be careful with what is in there.'

So, Zippy started to search in the suitcase. He was into the contents, nose working, and feet planted firmly in the case as he moved about. A thorough job, but one that was causing the passenger some disquiet: not because he had anything to hide, but because he was concerned about the proximity of the dog's paws and his shiny laptop. Tony could see him flinching every time Zippy's claws came close to the laptop lid, and several times he looked as though he would be unable to resist leaning forward and trying to push the dog away.

'Please, tell him to be careful,' the man muttered more than once, each time a little more worried for his laptop. It was looking very much by now as though he had nothing to hide, but had a concern about his property being damaged. Unfortunately, he was to let this concern overrule anything he had been told...

The thing to remember about Zippy – and this is true of any dog to an extent, but some more than others, and Zippy was in the 'some' category – is that when he was in the middle of a search in a box, or case, or inside a cupboard, that was HIS property. At that moment, he owned that, and no-one else was allowed to get anywhere near it, or they would soon know about it. Because of this, Tony was keeping a careful eye on Zippy as he went about his work, and an even more careful eye on the passenger.

It was almost inevitable that something would happen: in the middle of searching through the case, Zippy stood on the laptop, and the slightest sound of his claw on the surface could be heard. It was nothing, but it was enough to make the jumpy passenger fear for his tech.

'Oh no–' Before Tony could stop him, or even warn him, the man jumped across from where he was standing and put his hand into the case. It was nothing more than a gesture to move the laptop and prevent damage, but in that moment, it was an ill-judged move.

Alert to someone encroaching on his property, Zippy turned round swiftly and bit him on the hand. It was just a nip, and not bad by any description, but nonetheless it was not a thing that any dog – let alone a police dog – should do. Especially in front of airport staff.

And just to make matters worse, it was confirmed that there was nothing in the case that was in any way illegal.

The airport security staff found it quite amusing. After all, it was the passenger's fault for putting his hand in the way when he shouldn't have done so. But at the same time, they told Tony that it didn't matter how funny they found it, it wasn't something that they could allow.

'Think what it would be like if someone decided to sue us every time that little bugger got narky with someone,' he was told.

And so, from that time on, they would not be able to let Zippy into the airport, even if he was the dog on call. Sorry, he was told, but the dog is effectively banned…

If that wasn't enough, Zippy was about to make it an even worse day for Tony…

As they were walking out of the airport, Tony wanted to give Zippy a bit of a reward for being a good dog. A good search dog. After all, he might have tried to take a chunk out of the man's hand, but he was only doing his duty, and the man was foolish to put his hand in when he had already been warned.

So, Tony decided to give the dog a treat and let him indulge in one of his favourite pastimes when he was in the airport. There was nothing he liked more than to wander up and down the lines of passengers checking in, just having a little sniff and checking them out. Of course, walking up and down the line like that with a dog made a few passengers look askance at Tony, but if they had nothing to hide, why would it bother them?

So, Tony took him up and down the line, not with any intent other than to let Zippy have a little sniff before he left. However, there was one man in the queue who looked a bit nervous as Zippy walked past.

'This guy had a holdall on the floor beside him. We walked past him, but Zippy pulled me back towards the holdall. He did this a couple of times, and I went to pull him away, but each time I did it he just got more insistent. It was one of those holdalls that had a zip pocket on one side, and Zip kept sniffing at it and then trying to paw and scratch at the pocket on the side. Each time that Zippy pulled me back, the man with the holdall started to look more and more sheepish and nervous.'

The last thing Tony wanted was any more trouble that day, but he also knew that when a dog is doing something like Zippy was right then, you were obliged as a police officer to follow it up. Because the dogs are trained to sniff out illicit items, so behaviour like this would surely mean there was something in there that shouldn't be…

The man whose holdall it was looked at Tony nervously and said, 'There's nothing in there.'

Tony tried to reassure him. 'Look, it's probably nothing, but as he's acting like this it does more or less oblige me to have a look. If you just open the holdall, let me see what's in there, then we can clear this up in a moment.'

The man reluctantly agreed, but as he picked it up, he said, 'There's nothing in there. Nothing that would interest the police.'

His behaviour was very odd: acting suspiciously yet at the

same time looking as though he were telling the truth. And his choice of words was also bizarre in the circumstances.

All Tony could say to him was 'Well, you can say that, but Zip's saying very differently by doing this…'

The man sighed. He knew the game was up: it was just that the game was not what Tony might have expected. He started to unzip the holdall, saying 'It's Walls'. Greeted by an uncomprehending stare, he continued, 'Sausages.'

'Are you having a game here?' Tony asked him. But looking down at Zippy, who was still excited by the scent he had picked up, he started to wonder. It sounded ridiculous, but could it be true? Not sure if it was true, Tony made the man unpack his holdall, still standing in the check-in queue. With a reluctance that can only be born out of acute embarrassment, the man unzipped the side pocket of the holdall and pulled out a pack of Walls' sausages. The packet had split open where it had been stuffed in, and so the sausages were releasing their uncooked, but still alluring to a dog, aroma.

Having been asked if he would care to explain, the man told Tony that he didn't like Spanish sausage. He was off on holiday, and couldn't face the fortnight without a sausage, but wouldn't consider one with garlic, paprika, or whatever else they put in that Walls left out. So, he had decided to take his own supplies, not realising that he had split the pack, and not reckoning on being passed by a sniffer dog with a nose for a sausage.

Tony found it hard to believe that Zippy could have sniffed them out just by passing by, but then when you consider the abilities that his sharp fox terrier nose had shown over the past few years, it's perhaps not that difficult to believe.

It made for quite a day: banned from the airport for nipping a laptop-loving passenger, and then sniffing out sausages and leaving another poor passenger shamefacedly unpacking his luggage and admitting his dislike of Spanish sausage in front a queue who thought they were having the thrill of seeing him busted for drugs. Which would have livened up their check in wait no end.

This is the reality of a working dog's life as much as it is of their handler. For every tense hostage situation, for every chase that ends up with the apprehension of a perpetrator, for every taut and anxious hunt for a missing person, there is the everyday grind of going through cars, houses, warehouses and sheds, suitcases, and bags. A grind that gets results some of the time, and some of the time can seem almost like farce.

People Are Strange...

THERE IS a lighter side to the job, and it makes the life of a handler one of constant surprises. This tends to be the case more with a specialist dog such as a sniffer rather than a general-purpose dog. The general-purpose dog, such as Taz, is deployed in more hazardous situations and more often. Storm, and then Kane, the other dogs that Tony had during Zippy's career, would have seen him as handler in some perilous situations. Zippy's career, like all sniffer dogs, was not without its hazards, but it did tend to lend itself by its very nature towards the more strange and bizarre.

A lot of house searches include the bedroom, and this is where things could get a little odd. Maybe it was just an Essex thing, or maybe it's common across the UK, but it seems that in many bedrooms across the county there was a storage box, usually hidden in the bottom of the wardrobe, where people would keep their sex toys and costumes for fetish or role-play.

'Whips, vibrators, gags, rubber, leather – any kind of sex aid, toy or fabric and material you could imagine,' Tony explained.

'The thing about these boxes was that they would also act as good hiding places, as people were also inclined to stuff their drugs in their boxes, thinking that no-one would think to search in there. Or would particularly want to go down there,' he added.

This is not great thinking. A sniffer dog loves smells, and in a box like that there will always be a lot of scents for a dog to find interesting. This was certainly the case with Zippy: he liked to have a really good sniff around any boxes like this and part of his job was to go there as there was no way a storage box would be left alone by any industrious police officer. Quite the opposite, given their common use as hiding places.

Zippy's behaviour around these boxes struck Tony sometimes as just being plain weird, in the same way that he had tried to mount Storm, it seemed as though the pheromones and smells from the boxes hit some remnant of the hormones that had been taken from him when he was neutered and triggered a reaction that Zippy himself couldn't really understand, but found compelling.

But his habits were not professional or good at this point. He was acting like a plain old dog rather than a professional sniffer dog. He would act in a very peculiar and particular way. Tony described it as 'very Beavis and Butthead', which those readers of a certain age will recognise immediately. A kind of strange, rictus smile at the jaw and a habit of breathing heavily with a 'heh-heh-heh' sound. It's a reaction the likes of which you can sometimes see in your own dog when out walking and it sniffs a marking scent left by another dog: the pheromones within the marker trigger a reaction in the dog picking it up. It looks perfectly natural when a dog does it in the wild, but perhaps not so much so when it does it in a suspect's bedroom.

The worst time that Tony can remember is when they were

searching a bedroom and Zippy was sniffing at the bed. 'I pulled back the covers and there was a strange, unidentifiable jelly-like brown puddle clustered in the middle of the sheets. I had no idea what it was and to be honest I didn't want to know. Trouble was, Zippy found it irresistible and jumped on the bed, burying his muzzle and rolling about in it. That was bad enough, but then I had to pick him up and carry him out. He looked disgusting covered in the brown gunk, and he didn't smell much better, either. It got a few remarks back at the station where that search operation was based...'

Maybe it was just as well that no-one else was aware of one of Zippy's other little habits. When he got over-excited and stimulated by those kinds of bedroom searches, he would pee over the pillows on the bed. It was only a marking pee, so not much. Looking discretely the other way, Tony would flip the pillow over and often wondered how many weeks after being turned over it would be before the owners of the bed realised that their pillow smelt a little funny.

If this paints a picture of a sniffer dog that you would perhaps not care to think about, it has to be born in mind that these are working dogs, working animals and that sometimes their animal instincts get the better of them, no matter how good the training. It's unfortunate but it's just a fact of life.

How To Get Injured By Your Own Team

ZIPPY WAS only ever injured twice in the time that Tony had him, and ironically neither was in the line of work, and both were accidents with other dogs. The first time has already been mentioned, when Storm took off the end of Zippy's ear. The other time entailed a more serious injury, and on that occasion Zippy ended up with 18 stitches and fragments of bone taken from his skull. The absurd thing about it was that it resulted from play between Zippy and Kane. How could their playing end up in such serious damage?

Quite easily, as it turns out. Zippy was a very small dog, whereas Kane was around 40 kilos. Therein lay the problem…

'At the end of the working day, I liked to let them both out of the back of the van and into a field. Some days they had been cooped up in the back for a considerable time, and it gave them a chance to exercise, stretch their muscles and let off some steam. What I would do is let them out, then throw a ball into the distance so they could hare off after it. On this particular day I did it and then turned away knowing that they would be circling around the flight of the ball, heading towards it from opposite directions like they always did.

What I didn't see was that they must have both run full pelt towards the ball as it landed and came head-to-head, colliding muzzle to muzzle. Kane carried on running, got the ball, and ran back to the van. It was only when I turned round, I could see that Zippy was standing in the middle of the field, where the ball had landed, and wasn't moving. Something was definitely wrong.'

Tony headed towards Zippy, who stood stock still. 'As I got nearer I could see that where they had collided and smashed heads together, Zip had come off worse. His eyeball had popped out and was just dangling down over his muzzle. He was starting to wobble as he stood there, and it was obvious that he was going into shock.'

Picking him up quickly, Tony ran back to the van. Kane was already in the back, and shutting that door Tony put Zippy in front with him. They were in the middle of a field, away from town, and he had very little with which to treat the dog, who was in real danger of going fully into shock and losing consciousness. Using a wound dressing from the first aid kit he did his best to get the eye back in the socket and wrap bandaging around his head to get it secured. As soon as this was done, he wrapped him up as best he could in the passenger seat and headed back towards the vet, using the blue light to clear the way ahead. Even as he drove, he could see Zippy start to shake as shock took hold of him. All you could really see of the dog was his nose sticking out of the bandages.

'When we reached the vet, I rushed him inside. I hoped the fact that Zippy was in shock would calm him down and enable him to be treated. Because he really hated the vet. When he had his yearly injections, the only way they could administer them to the yowling, biting ball of fury that he was in a surgery was for me to take hold of him and pin up against a wall, holding him in place until the injection had been administered. I had to grab him and hold him up by his chest, back against the wall, so that he couldn't bite and his legs were pinned.'

If Tony was hoping that pain and shock would make anything like this unnecessary on this occasion, he was sadly mistaken. As they went inside, he could feel Zippy start to twitch and look around. It was as if you could hear him thinking 'hang on, where am I? Oh no, not here…' It was going to be a race between sedating him and the dog coming out of shock enough to start kicking off at where he was.

It was a race that Tony won, pinning Zippy down while he was injected and sedated, so they were able to operate on him and put his eye back in place. But once he came round, that was another story: originally, the vet planned to keep him in for a couple of days.

'By the end of the following day they called me up and said I would have to come and pick him up. Please come and get him, in fact: once he had come round, he had been a terrible patient even in his cage, and the vet's staff hadn't been able to get near him. I did say to them that I wasn't a vet and wouldn't know what to do, but he'd been so disruptive that they were happy to give me instructions and let me get on with it.'

Tony still has the glass pot he was given which had the six or seven pieces of bone that were taken out of Zippy's skull when he was opened up. The force of his collision with Kane had been so great that it had shattered part of his skull and cheekbone. His tear duct was damaged so that he had a permanently watering eye from that time onwards. His head had been shaved and he had a ruff of fur as well as a buster collar to stop him worrying at his stitches. These stitches presented another problem: they had to be removed.

'I took him back to the vet, but she couldn't get near him. There was no way that anyone was going to get near those stitches without any damage. The vet decided that she would have to sedate him again…' Tony got him pinned up in the corner of the surgery, against the wall, but as the vet tried to get past, she caught Tony's arm with the needle. 'Careful, it's the dog you're supposed to be sedating, not me, I told her. The last thing she needed was me passing out and Zip wide awake.'

But even trying to sedate Zippy didn't work, and eventually the vet asked Tony if he thought he could get the stitches out. 'Well, I've never done that before, but he will let me do anything to him,' he told her. And so he did: Tony was able to remove the stitches where no-one else could get near.

It is true that Tony was the only one who could actually do anything with Zippy, and the dog would let him.

'That is what he was like. He followed me everywhere. He was like my shadow. Everywhere I went, I would turn round and Zippy would be there.'

The dog absolutely adored him, but wasn't exactly keen on anyone else.

If You're Not My Handler...

THIS WAS proved to the public when there was an open day at the kennels one year. The dogs in the dog section were penned in cages or out on display for the public to come and see them.

'With all those dogs there was only one visitor bitten during the whole day: a young girl, who put her fingers into Zippy's cage without asking him. It was her own fault in one way,' Tony adds.

And it wasn't just the public who could incur his displeasure. 'There was one old police inspector, a very straight and upright copper of the old school. I would often take Zippy to the station with me, and he would follow me around the offices. This was not that usual, mostly because there were rarely dogs small enough to walk around the offices without getting in the way. There's just not enough room for one like Storm, or Kane. Anyway, this inspector asked if he could make a fuss of Zippy and just say hello to him. The problem was, Zippy was not in the mood for it that day, and next thing I knew, he'd not just had a snap at the inspector, but had chased him across the office as he tried to retreat, just to let him know who was boss.'

On another occasion, while they were searching a caravan, one of the officers in charge was not a dog handler, but actually a man who disliked dogs immensely. All the while they were searching the caravan he kept saying to Tony, 'You are keeping him on a lead, aren't you?'

Fed up with this and knowing that others on the search would enjoy it, he decided that he would wind up this officer. It was particularly Zippy that he was afraid of – small dog, big reputation – and Tony knew that there were particular commands that this officer did not know, but to which Zippy would respond.

Once the search was completed, he took Zippy to the caravan where the officer was discussing matters with a colleague. Tony left Zippy in there, remarking 'watch him, watch him now for me while he's free,' and went out. The officer was now cornered and afraid to move while Zippy looked at him quizzically, waiting for his next command, with everyone else watching along with Tony through the windows of the caravan.

This little dog's big reputation would often precede him amongst the police of Essex, and it's true that Zippy was a tough nut. But he was also highly disciplined and trained. He knew his job and he loved his job. He knew what he had to do as a sniffer dog, but also liked to have a real, regular dog's life of chasing, scrapping, and chasing balls.

Like most police dogs, he had some experience of a helicopter, but unlike most for this he was put in a pet tube, made of Gore-Tex with a mesh on one end, which Tony would also use when he had to put Zippy in his own car. Not many police dogs are small enough for a pet carrier, and it certainly looked strange enough when Tony had him in it: the handles made it look as though Tony was carrying his dog around in a handbag...

Zippy Retires

ZIPPY STARTED his serving life in 2005 and was operational for seven years. Tony then retired him home as he had reached the optimum age for police dog retirement, having passed eight years old. He settled in at home for a while, and when Tony's son was born, he would lay on the playmat with the baby and look after him like he'd looked after Tony. But when he reached toddler age, the boy wanted to play with Zippy and, like most children, could be unintentionally heavy-handed. Like most dogs, Zippy was fine with this and showed no sign of being bothered by it. Occasionally there would be the odd low growl if it got too much, but no sign of anything else. And as I can attest from my own dog and grandchildren, the growl is nothing more than a quiet moan.

But Tony knew that Zippy was not the kind of dog who liked to be pawed, and as his son obviously knew no better at that age, there was a chance it could not end well. By this time, Zippy was well into the senior stage and had lost a lot of his bottom and top teeth, though he still had his canines. Enough to still give a nasty nip if pushed too far. It led to a decision Tony had never wanted to make, and still sounds sad about to this day.

'It's not one I ever wanted to make, but I decided that Zippy would have to spend his last few years having been rehomed. I knew I had to be sensible and not put either my son or Zippy in a position that would be bad for both of them: I followed my head though my heart was telling me otherwise.'

He kept Kane, as he was still a working dog. Zippy was rehomed with a woman named Sue, who gave him a family so good that he was able to adjust even without his beloved Tony. It also proved that even Zippy could mellow with age. He had a very happy retirement, and Tony was reunited with him again when, a little while later, he received his retired dog's service medal in a ceremony at county headquarters.

'By this time Zippy was quite chilled, and I was able to sneak up behind him and pick him up. It took him by surprise and he looked around, ready to kick off – still – and it was only when I said hello to him that he realised who I was. He went mad with excitement, overjoyed to see me again. He had no teeth, was going blind, and was deaf, but for a moment he was the Zippy I knew.'

He was 17 when he peacefully passed away.

Life After The Zipster

TONY, MEANWHILE, continued as a handler. Kane had by then retired, and he had a new general-purpose dog called Will, as well as a new sniffer who was a spaniel. He worked with it for a while, but in the end, he couldn't get on with the spaniel.

'It was a messy dog and upset the kennel where there were three dogs. The other two would keep one part of the kennel as a toilet, but the spaniel would mess anywhere, even in his food bowl. He was hyperactive and tipped things over. His hyperactivity made him hard to train.' And he wasn't Zippy. Coming after such a character, it was always going to be hard for Tony to adjust to a new sniffer, let alone one with behavioural issues. Eventually, he had the dog retrained and allocated to another handler, where with a different environment he was able to work for several years. Tony waited a few years before getting another specialist dog, this one being trained to sniff for drugs.

What Made This 'Scruffy Little Mutt' Special?

Of course, it's not just about the trainers and handlers – it's the dog that does the job, and some dogs have an advantage that others just don't have. The one thing that most specialist dogs didn't have that Zippy had in his favour was his size. The problem with a big specialist dog, as we have seen in this chapter, is size. Cars are a perfect example of this. It's difficult for a big dog to get into all the areas of a car with ease. However, with Zippy: 'I knew I could just pop Zippy into a car and he would be in the footwells and under the dash, between the seats and along the well at the back, and then over into the boot with no problem, as he was small enough to just fit into these spaces.'

He was so good at the job that he gave Tony absolute confidence in his ability to carry out any search well.

'It made him fun to work with as he could go into a room and you knew within a minute if you were going to find something. Give him the run of a room and before you started the detailed search, he would know if there was something there. You could sense it from his body language. It didn't matter whether it was anything big or anything small, you'd immediately know that there was something in that room that Zippy would find. On the other hand, if there wasn't anything there, he'd be completely switched off, just as if you had turned a key. He would jog around, not bothered with anything. He wouldn't switch on at all.'

Of course, Tony would still go back to run a search properly, but if it was done in great detail and the room pulled apart, if Zippy hadn't been switched on, you would know that you'd come away with nothing. So, he gave Tony that confidence in his own ability in the job.

Zippy always carried on working and he never switched off unless there was nothing to find. Often, as part of retraining and as part of keeping training up, a handler will use distractions such as food, other dogs, toys - anything to try and distract the dog from the search. Zippy could never be distracted: he had complete and utter focus.

Zippy's Gone, But The Legend Lives On

ZIPPY WAS, for many years, the star of a poster that was in the police college in Witham, which can't be said of many dogs. When they were arranging photo shoots for the posters that are used in the building, the photographers asked if they could shoot one of the dogs actually carrying out a search.

Tony was asked about Zippy, and he agreed. But when they came down to do the filming, he made sure that he slipped on Zippy's harness and prepared him when they were both out of sight, as he knew what the reaction would be. Sure enough, as he walked round the corner to the car they had set up for the shoot, he could see by their faces that they were not impressed.

So, he said, 'Oh well, if that's how it is I'll just put him back.'

With no other option on show, they reluctantly agreed, grumbling that it was not what they expected. But nonetheless, the picture taken with Zippy in harness going to work against the side of a car was more than good enough to go on the poster. And often, detectives from where Tony was stationed would go on courses at the college, come back and remark that they'd seen Zippy down there, because that poster was up there for years, long after he retired from service.

A strong character and a great working dog never gets forgotten by other officers, and even now when episodes of 'Police Interceptors' that feature Zippy turn up on TV, Tony gets texts from people he hasn't seen for a long time who remember Zippy, with fondness or trepidation, depending on whether or not they incurred his ire.

Tony finished our talk about Zippy by remarking that he knew how good he would be from the very beginning: 'I went on a two months drug sniffing course with him. There were two spaniels on the course, and only one survived the duration as the other was just not good enough and bombed out in the early weeks.'

On the course, they set up small searches which tell us a lot about the training for drug dogs in recent years. 'The dogs searched for very tiny, small amounts of drugs. They should have been able to detect even the slightest trace. Cigarette filter papers were soaked in drugs overnight. They weren't left wet, but were dried out, still retaining the smell. These would be rolled up and squeezed in-between locker drawers, in the cracks between these drawers, and in similar small cracks in furniture. They were put in place with tweezers. There's no obvious smell, but enough of a chemical scent for the dog to pick up. The dog and handler who were training would be let into the room, and they would not know where the drugs were located. A large variety of drugs were used from cocaine to heroin, MDMA to ketamine, right down to the easily detected scents like cannabis. The dog would then blindly have to search around the room and find them.'

Zippy had no trouble with any of this. He did cash with ease. He did guns and ammunition: it was here that Tony thought Zippy might perhaps fail, if only because he'd been so good that he thought sooner or later he was bound to slip up. But even with these, as Zippy's prowess with a pallet showed earlier, he had no problem. Zippy was just amazing at his job.

Did he have any faults? Tony considered this before saying there were no faults in his work, but maybe one drawback.

'The only thing that could perhaps be said to let him down compared to, say, a spaniel, was because he was a smaller dog. He didn't have the stamina of a larger animal. But this could be compensated easily: you simply did smaller stints of work. A dog would, on average, work a stint of 10 to 20 minutes before being rested. Zippy would work a slightly lesser amount of time and have a break in-between. With that minor adjustment his ability never faltered, and his stamina was controlled. If he had the right breaks, you got the same results.

'You could just pick him up, put him in places, and he was "Yep, done it". And you just got to think, this is nice. Now, it's good to work like this because you'd go somewhere and if you had a car or somewhere to search, you would just pop him in. He'd be jumping over the back seat, and he'd be under and over, and it was just so simple. He always worked. He never failed.'

In truth, every dog that has ever served is worthy of such a tribute. They all play their part, and they are all remarkable, resourceful, brave, and smart animals.

Epilogue

THE FUTURE OF POLICE DOGS

THE RESPONSIBILITY for the standards of training has been maintained for some years now by the National Police Chiefs Council, who issue documents outlining their expectations for trainers and handlers.

The 2024 Police Dog Training Standard v1 outlines appropriate methods of training for police dogs in a formal setting, an informal setting, and whilst being deployed. It is directed towards dog handlers, trainers, kennel staff and any personnel involved with police dog training, as well as any management that have responsibility for training. It applies to any dog that is undergoing initial or continuation training, husbandry (breeding of police dogs), training in operational areas, and any other formal or informal training in any setting. The handler is responsible for this whether on or off duty. Put simply, it entrusts everyone involved with dogs to maintain the standards set.

It states that all forces have individual policies, procedures, and risk assessments in relation to training of their police dogs. The purpose of the document is to assist instructors during training and behaviour modification, giving them guidelines for any decisions. There's a paper called the National Decision Model which has to be utilised at all times.

To have such a nationalised standard approach means that all trainers and handlers are reading off the same page, and allows for a standard to be set that is consistent. When you look at the history of dog section development as we have seen in these pages, it's pretty obvious that the hierarchies in some forces were a whole lot better at understanding how dogs can be used, and how they can best be accommodated, than others.

It defines training as whenever a police dog is given a comment, either verbal such as sit, down, or wait; or physical, such as pulling on lead, and an outcome is desired or expected. It demands that all staff must be trained and competent in ensuring there is a good provision for the safe handling and the welfare of the dog.

Under this standard, staff are expected to document their continuing professional development in a portfolio which can be examined to ensure that they are either trained to the correct standard for any requirements of their role, or are in the process of further training to attain that level. This ensures that any dogs that are in deployment or are in their initial training are in the hands of competent and informed handlers and trainers, and so their training will equip them for the tasks they are expected to perform.

Interestingly, it goes on to state that a correct preparation for the training environment will limit the number of mistakes made with (by handlers and trainers) and by the dogs, but the trainer or handler should not expect the dog to be perfect: mistakes should be expected and anticipated during training by reading the behaviour of the dog, and any errors and mistakes should be seen as an opportunity to improve the learning and competence of the dog. Reading the behaviour of the dog: meaning that the expectation is for handlers to learn as much from the dog as the dog learns from them.

This should be something that everyone involved in the care and training of dogs adopts, as positive reinforcement is a pre-requisite of successful dog training. As this always involves repetition – the constant use of the ball to imprint and enforce the task being taught, for example – then the more the dog understands and predicts the result of its behaviour, the more reliable that will become. Limiting any confusion in a dog is the prime responsibility of all those involved in the training and care of police dogs.

It's worth noting that there was no confusion shown in the behaviour of Major, or indeed of Taz, Rex III and Zippy. They were dogs that always knew what they were doing. In part this was because of the standards that were developed in the years before this 2024 document, which it tries to encapsulate for future handlers and trainers; but in part it was also because the trainers learned from the intelligence and reaction of the dog. The standard makes it seem one way, but the dog has, by the very behaviours the document talks about, helped to define those standards in what is a very symbiotic relationship.

The one thing that comes across when reading the standard is the emphasis is on the handler and trainer: I know what you're thinking, it's obvious that it would be as if the dog can't read… But leaving that aside, it's very strong on the idea that the handler and trainer must have a clear idea of what it is they wish for the dog to achieve from specific commands, and the kind of reinforcement action they take to reward the dog for its success. From the years when trainers seemed to leave handlers to work out what they should do to train their dogs and how they should handle them, we now have a clearly defined framework that is there not only to ensure the welfare and the efficiency of the dog, but also give the humans a clear pathway for what they should be aiming for, and how they should achieve this.

This is important, as almost all handlers are diligent in their job, if individualistic, but there have always been those few (as in any profession) who have had a sense of duty that can be questioned. You only have to think back to Arthur Holman's shock at being told on a night call-out that he was the fourth handler to be called, and the only one to respond. That was seven decades ago, and even in the time of Major not all handlers were as dedicated as Allan Beddoe. The aim of this standard is to weed out those few if they don't keep to its demands.

It's no more than the dogs deserve.

Where would we be without them?

Acknowledgements

A BOOK LIKE this does not write itself. Thank you to Clare Fitzsimons and Christine Costello, my editor, and the team at Mirror books. To Tom Cull, my agent at Cull and Co.

Special thanks to Elaine Michaels and Tony Mayo for sharing their stories and pictures of Taz and Zippy with me.

Thank you to Anita Holman (and Rambo) for being there, and for her help in research.

Particular thanks for help with contacts, advice and support to Linda Belgrove of the Association Of Retired Police Dog Charities, who has been instrumental in helping pull this book together.

My thanks for help and advice to Lady B, Countess Bathurst, of the National Foundation For Retired Service Animals, and for her foreword.

If you have any interest in what happens to dogs when they retire, beyond what you have read in this book, then please visit the two sites listed below. Police Forces across the country are stretched for funding every year, and so do not have the pockets necessary to provide for dogs when they have to retire. This is where the Foundation and also the Retired Police Dog Charities across the country step in: help with rehoming, with hardship, with ongoing medical costs, all of this they aim to cover. They can only do this because of fundraising and the generosity of those who care what happens to dogs when they leave the service because of age or injury.

The National Foundation For Retired Service Animals: https://www.nfrsa.org.uk/

The Association Of Retired Police Dog Charities: http://www.associationofretiredpolicedogcharities.uk/

On the first page of the latter, you will find links to all the charities across the regions.

The K9 Memorial UK can be found at https://www.k9memorialuk.co.uk/, where you will find details of their fundraising. To quote from their site: 'In the UK, to commemorate the valuable role carried out by police dogs, a plaque is sited within the Police Memorial Garden at the National Memorial Arboretum in Staffordshire.

We have also raised funds for a more suitable and fitting sculpture in memory of the many dogs who have played such a valuable role within the police service and given their lives to help keep our communities safe. The Memorial is situated in the grounds of Oaklands Park, Chelmsford, Essex. The K9 Memorial is responsible for creating the United Kingdom's first Police Dog retirement medal.'